THE

MILLIONAIRE

COURSE

BY MARC ALLEN

BOOKS
The Ten Percent Solution:
Simple Steps to Improving Our Lives and Our World

Visionary Business:
An Entrepreneur's Guide to Success

A Visionary Life:
Conversations on Personal and Planetary Evolution

How to Think like a Millionaire
(with Mark Fisher)

A Two-Second Love Affair (Poetry)

AUDIOCASSETTES
Stress Reduction and Creative Meditations

Stress Reduction and Creative Meditations for
Work and Career

Visionary Business: An Entrepreneur's Guide to Success
(Complete book on audio)

MUSIC
Solo Flight

Breathe

Petals

THE
MILLIONAIRE
COURSE

A Visionary Plan for Creating
the Life of Your Dreams

MARC ALLEN

NEW WORLD LIBRARY
NOVATO, CALIFORNIA

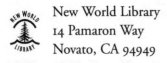 New World Library
14 Pamaron Way
Novato, CA 94949

Editing: Yvette Bozzini and Chris Cone
Cover design: Mary Ann Casler
Text design: Tona Pearce Myers
Author photo: Michael Collopy

Library of Congress Cataloging-in-Publication Data
Allen, Mark, 1946–
The millionaire course : a visionary plan for creating the life of your dreams / Marc Allen.
    p.   cm.
Includes bibliographical references and index.
  ISBN 1-57731-232-5 (pbk. : alk. paper)
  1. Success. I. Title.
  BJ1611.2 .A46 2003
  158.1—dc21   002153768

First printing, April 2003
ISBN 1-57731-232-5
Printed in Canada on acid-free, partially recycled paper
Distributed to the trade by Publishers Group West

10   9   8   7

This book is dedicated

to all of you

who have the courage to dream.

CONTENTS

FOREWORD

BY SHAKTI GAWAIN

When I first met Marc Allen, he had literally no money. We were both living in a spiritual community where we worked in exchange for room, board, and basic expenses but earned no other money. Marc's first task every morning was to figure out a way to get a dollar to buy a latte. Somehow, he always succeeded.

Marc was a musician, an actor, and a writer. Like many artists and most spiritually oriented people, he cared little about money and knew nothing about saving or managing it. Yet somehow in his unique, relaxed way, he always seemed to draw to him exactly what he needed.

Fast forward to a couple of years later: Marc and I had both left the community, and we had each written books on personal growth that we were trying to figure out how to get published. So we borrowed a little money from friends and family and published them ourselves. That was the beginning of New World Library.

Over the years I have seen Marc grow into personal, artistic, and financial success as a publisher and an author. He has had a positive impact on a great many people, including me.

He always seems to be so relaxed and easy going, never in a hurry, always having time for friends and family, time to pet the cat or play a little music. And yet he has written some powerful books and, with persistence and patience, created one of the finest publishing companies in the world today.

When he wrote *Visionary Business* in 1995, his impact grew into the business world. The book and his ongoing mentoring helped countless individuals and businesses to realize their dreams.

Now, with *The Millionaire Course,* his impact is extending more broadly to reach a wide range of people who are serious about positively changing their lives and the world. I can vouch for the fact that Marc has practiced exactly what he preaches in this book and it has worked for him on all levels. Don't be fooled by his low-key, understated style. This book is filled with practical wisdom that can help you create a fulfilled life.

— Shakti Gawain
Author of *Creative Visualization*

· ·

BY TOM CHAVEZ

These days, when we read a daily paper or watch the news, we're struck with a certain cold reality: *You almost need to be a millionaire to just get by!* We never know what's going to happen or what an unexpected emergency might cost — even good insurance doesn't completely protect us. It takes a small fortune to put a child through a good school, and far too many people can't even afford to buy their own homes. What used to be considered great wealth — a million dollars in assets — is now something that a vast number of us would like simply for the security and comfort it can bring us and our families.

The Millionaire Course was created to do just that. Taking this Course can bring us the kind of results that our dreams are made of: having time and resources and freedom to enjoy life, having power and authority, and — best of all — finding personal fulfillment.

The nation, and apparently most of the world, is infatuated with the wealthy, and most people dream the great *What if....* We need only witness the phenomena of big-buck quiz shows and lottery-mania. The chances of you and me becoming a millionaire via these processes are well documented — several-million-to-one at best.

But what if, just *what if,* there was a definite, specific, proven set of principles that, if followed, could help us live the life of our dreams? And what if we could achieve our highest goals and dreams by doing what we love to do, while adhering to compassionate, conscious values?

This is exactly what this Course can do for anyone who is willing to commit to the program — to study it, to plan, and to act on that plan. This Course not only puts you on the right track philosophically and psychologically, it goes on to give you the real tools — the business plan, the vocabulary, even resources for financing — that you'll need to complete the job. This is not simply a set of motivational ideas; it is precisely what it says it is: *a visionary guide to creating the life of your dreams.*

This Course was created by a bona fide self-made multimillionaire who created his wealth using the principles he so clearly explains in this book. He draws from a great many resources, including every book and speaker that has had a major influence on his life and career; he refers repeatedly to some of the greatest entrepreneurial and motivational minds in history, men and women who inspired him and who will inspire you to develop a true visionary view of the vast potential of your own being.

Your instructor in this Course, Marc Allen, calls his approach "visionary business." He walks his talk, applying these visionary principles to the company he founded and built, New World Library, which has published an impressive collection of works by Eckhart Tolle, Shakti Gawain, Deepak Chopra, Riane Eisler, Barbara Marx Hubbard, Joseph

Campbell, Dan Millman, Alan Watts, James Allen, Kent Nerburn, Richard Carlson, and many others.

He is the author of *Visionary Business, A Visionary Life, The Ten Percent Solution,* and co-author of *How to Think like a Millionaire.* He is an inspiring speaker, and has appeared nationally on TV, radio, and in his seminars presenting these life-changing concepts.

With the right tools, there are no limits to what you can achieve. It's all here, minus one ingredient: *your creative mind.* Here is everything else you need — so let's get on with the business of realizing our greatest dreams.

— Tom Chavez
CEO, Visionary Communications, Inc.

THE

. . . .

MILLIONAIRE

. . . .

COURSE

What is a deeply satisfying human life,
and how do we design one?

How do we share that information with each other?
What are we here to do together,
and what are we truly capable of
in the realm of human excellence?

The answers to these questions
are not mysteries beyond our reach.
Fulfillment of the promise
of our soul's nature is possible.
It is why we are here. It is our birthright.
The answers are found in the inner frontiers of Being.

— Lenedra J. Carroll
The Architecture of All Abundance

. . . .

BY MARC ALLEN

WELCOME TO AN ADVENTURE

As I slowly discovered the material in this Course, my life changed completely. My twenties had been marked by struggle and poverty. I felt a nearly constant level of anxiety and periods of depression. By the time I was in my mid- to late thirties, however, life had become an adventure, filled with discovery. My anxiety and depression had evaporated, transformed into a deep sense of peace and gratitude and even wonder. It is not an exaggeration to say that miracles and magic happened when I began to use the tools in this Course — the gifts from a great many generous mentors, teachers, authors, and others. I am filled with a sense of gratitude for the life I have created (with the help of my friends), and for all I have been given. I do what I love to do, and the world supports me with endless abundance.

The best part of the adventure is that I've found it is something I can pass on to others. Within this book is an adventure you design yourself, for you will quickly see how to plan your own course. That's what makes it so satisfying and meaningful: It is an adventure of your own making. You choose the destination, and the route as well. Along the way, it stretches your imagination in endless fascinating ways, and improves your life in a countless number of ways.

Along the way you discover many keys. Many of them you have known for a long time; some of them you've perhaps already put to good use. This Course is a set of keys to the greatest adventure of all, for it gives us the tools to chart our own unique path, to create and live the life of our dreams.

Where do these keys come from? The answer is a key in itself:

KEY 2   ***Keys to success are everywhere.***

This book is filled with keys. Our lives, once we see it, are filled with keys. They're all around us, everywhere we look. A river running through a forest, a purring cat, even the plant on your windowsill can show you how to live your life. A comment from a friend, a few words on the radio, part of a quote in a book or on the internet, even a fragment of a commercial can give you a key that can change your life.

When I look back on the winding path of my life's adventure, I realize that one of the most important things I did along the way was to take certain key phrases I heard or read and repeat them, over and over, and reflect on them. Over time, they become imprinted in memory, and come to mind in all kinds of situations in daily life, and become invaluable creative guidance, regardless of the circumstances.

I invite you to do the same, and see the results. Even if you're skeptical about the whole process, just try it as a worthwhile experiment, and see what happens in your life. Take any phrase from this Course that appeals to you in some way — many are highlighted in bold type — and repeat it, remember it, live with it for a while, and see how you can apply it in your life.

These phrases have become words that guide me, and my life has changed dramatically as a result.

A GREAT KEY

Many of these keys are illusive, or baffling. Many seem simplistic, or obvious. Many are very much like Zen *koans* — cryptic little phrases that need to be meditated on before they are understood.

Here's a great one we've all heard:

Work smarter, not harder.   KEY 3

We've heard it a hundred times: Is it part of our life experience? Do we practice it? This is a good question to ask yourself: Are you working hard or working smart? Reading this book is certainly a step in the right direction.

Here's another one we've all heard before: *When life gives you lemons, make lemonade.* That little phrase is a great key to success, and we cover it in depth in Lesson Four. The title to that lesson is another key: *See the full half of the glass, the benefits in adversity, and keep picturing success.* The title of every lesson in this Course is a key in itself.

Children's songs, games, and stories are full of keys. *"Row, row, row your boat, gently down the stream, merrily, merrily, merrily, merrily, life is but a dream."* That song has great insight and understanding. Those words are a key to a life well lived.

There are keys in common phrases we often say to each other: *"Take it easy,"* we say — how many of us really do it? Those words are great advice for us all, every moment of our lives. Take it easy.

One of the most powerful keys I ever discovered was simply a little exercise in imagining:

KEY 4

> *You can create what you want in life;*
> *first you have to imagine it clearly.*
> *Imagine your ideal scene.*

This is a great key, and it's simply a little writing exercise: Put your "ideal scene" in writing. This, for some mysterious reason, is a powerful process that helps us go a long way toward creating that ideal scene in our lives. We go into this in detail in Lesson 1.

YOU DESIGN YOUR OWN COURSE

You decide which part to work on, and you do it in your own way, according to your own impulses. This Course is multifaceted, offering you a wide variety of ways to create what you want in life.

One of the best ways to work with this material is to go through the series of twelve chapters or lessons step-by-step, and then go back and roam through the material, pick out what you want to focus on, and work with it more extensively. But you don't necessarily have to work through the whole Course first to benefit from it, and if you're drawn at any time to focus on one particular lesson, or even just one particular key, do that. Follow your own impulses; work with it in your own way. Take as much or as little time with each lesson as you need.

There are three stages in learning:

1. First you have to hear or read the information, with enough receptiveness so that you take it in.

2. Then you have to reflect on it, and discover its meaning within your own experience. At this stage, information becomes knowledge.

3. Then you find new and creative ways you can apply it in your life, moment by moment, as challenges and opportunities arise. At this stage, knowledge has become wisdom.

Please put this book down every once in a while and reflect on what you have read. Apply it to your own life. It will be worth doing.

YOU DON'T HAVE TO DO IT ALL

Each of us is obviously different and unique. Find what works for you, and take it and freely adapt it as much as you choose. If there are parts of this Course you simply can't relate to, just skip over them and go on to the next thing, or go back and review in greater depth something you worked on previously.

This Course is a vast buffet of different choices and widely varied possibilities, and you certainly don't have to do everything recommended in this entire book. Nothing is required; everything is optional. As they say in Alcoholics Anonymous and other Twelve-Step programs, *"Take what you need and leave the rest."*

If you are even just a tiny bit open-minded — even if there is just a small crack in the hard shell of your current set of beliefs — there will be a moment when you suddenly see different and brighter possibilities in front of you, and you'll discover something of great value that will improve the quality of your life in a meaningful way.

You don't have to complete the whole Course before this

happens. You don't have to accept everything in the Course, either. If you don't relate to the "spiritual" content, for example, just go on to something else. I have included it because I have included everything that has affected me deeply enough to change my life, and many of those things are spiritual. I have learned about the power of prayer, and have seen its effects in my life. I have found that prayer, when done consistently, is a highly efficient, effective tool for growth and success. If because of your own particular background and vocabulary you don't choose to pray, or can't even relate to the concept of prayer, that's fine. Discover the power of affirmations instead, or self-suggestion, or creative visualization, or self-hypnosis, or reprogramming, or simply writing your goals repeatedly, or whatever else appeals to you. All these techniques work.

I do believe that if you're a spiritual person who has discovered prayer (to someone or something), it is far easier to create the kind of life you want, because it's such a direct, simple path: You pray, you let go — and prepare yourself to receive. Then the magic happens.

Pray, let go, and be ready to receive — this should be centered in bold, because it too is a powerful key, but I don't want to introduce too much spiritual material too fast. You don't need to be a "spiritual" person at all to make this Course work wonders for you.

In fact, you don't need to be anyone other than exactly who you are, for this Course makes it clear that you already have the tools you need to succeed in life — it's just a matter of using what you have more effectively.

KEY 5   *You have everything you need:*
a miraculous body, a phenomenal brain,
and a vast and powerful subconscious mind.

*Now it's just a matter of focusing them
in the right direction.*

THE KEYS TO SUCCESS ARE IN YOUR HANDS

Many of these keys are just simple, common sense. Many have the effect of reprogramming your conscious mind, creating new synapses in your brain, and deleting old programs that are not serving you or the world.

Many of these keys give you tools to deal with the doubts and fears that inevitably come up when you want to change and grow, expand into new levels of enjoyment and success, and live the life you've only fantasized about before.

There isn't just one key or secret to success. There are a great number of them, and I have tried to include in these pages every one that has had a major impact on my life.

These keys are often called secrets, and they remain secrets to most people, yet they are secrets not because anyone is trying to keep them from anyone else — in fact, successful people love spouting them. But they are *"self-secret,"* because their meaning is obscure until you discover it within your own mind, and apply it in your own experience.

A great many of these keys are well-known parts of the perennial philosophy that is as old as humankind. The ancient classic from India, the *Bhagavad Gita,* put it this way:

*I use the word secrets
not because these things are hidden,
but because so few people are prepared
to hear them today.*

KEY 6

— The Bhagavad Gita

That was written five thousand years ago — perhaps there are more people prepared to hear them today. Perhaps you're one of them. Find any phrase in this book, any key or secret that appeals to you at the moment, and think about it, repeatedly. Reflect on it, see how it can apply in your life. Have fun with it, too — the experience can be deeply satisfying as well as highly rewarding.

Many of these keys are set large on their own pages. Take a key that speaks to you and make a copy of it and put it on your wall where you see it often. Or write it on a business card or slip of paper and carry it around with you. Or put it on your mirror, on your refrigerator — anywhere you will keep being reminded of it — until what it has to teach you becomes part of your life.

Then you'll have a sudden moment of understanding, a bit of illumination, and you'll come to understand that "secret" to success in a new, fresh way — and you'll find a key to a whole new world, one with far greater possibilities.

Eventually you will come to fully understand:

KEY 7

You are a powerful, creative person,
able to do, be, and have what you want in life;
able to do what you love,
and to do it in your own way.

This is the promise of this Course. It is a course in creating the life of your dreams. It is a course in wealth creation — if that is part of your dream — and, more important, in your fulfillment as a human being, whatever that means to you.

What else is wealth for, other than supporting ourselves and others in realizing our dreams, our greatest potential? If wealth is not used for our good and for the good of others, it is empty, stagnant, and meaningless.

A LIFE-CHANGING KEY

One of the most powerful, life-changing keys I ever encountered was in a short little book written in 1904: *As You Think* — originally titled *As a Man Thinketh* — by James Allen, an English writer (who is no relation). I wrote many of the phrases in that book in big letters and put them on my wall in front of my desk. I carried some of them around with me in my pockets, and pulled them out and reflected on them occasionally during the day.

After a while, these words became imprinted in my memory and etched in my soul — and great changes began to happen in my life. This remains one of my favorite keys to ponder from *As You Think:*

> *You will become as great*
> *as your dominant aspiration....*
> *If you cherish a vision, a lofty ideal in your heart,*
> *you will realize it.*

KEY 8

> — James Allen, *As You Think*

Think about those words for a while. An important part of understanding it, for me, is in that word *dominant.* Our aspiration, our dream, has to be repeated so often it becomes more dominant than all the fears and doubts that naturally arise as soon as we have that dream, for our fears and doubts can prevent the realization of our dreams.

This is a great key to success. A dream seems so ethereal, insubstantial, and can so easily be forgotten — yet when a dream is remembered often enough, it has a way of becoming more substantial than all your doubts and fears about it. At some point along the way, that ephemeral dream can become a lasting *intention* — and then doors open, opportunities arise, you take the next obvious step and, in its own perfect time, your dream becomes a reality.

Don't take my word for it. Try it for yourself. Don't take any of this material lightly — I have helped countless people succeed in life, and I have helped a great many people become millionaires (including myself). We'll meet some of them in this Course and hear their stories. We are absolutely no different from you. It's just a matter of discovering certain simple tools and applying them in our lives. All the tools you need — in fact, far more tools than you'll ever need — are in this Course.

CREATING YOUR OWN COURSE

The Millionaire Course consists of twelve lessons. Each one is filled with keys to reflect on, and many of them give you something to write, something to add to your own condensed version of this Course that you're encouraged to make for yourself, step by step, piece by piece.

I strongly recommend that you get a notebook or binder of some kind — it can just be a folder with pockets, or even a file folder — so you can do some of the exercises in writing and add those pages to your binder or folder. Eventually, you'll create your own personalized version of this Course. I did this years ago, and feel it was probably the single most powerful step I ever took to create the success of my dreams. The same may be true for you as well.

I started with a folder with pockets in it; I wrote on the cover words that became a self-fulfilling affirmation: *I am now creating the life I want.*

After several years, it evolved into a simple file folder I called various names over the years: Prosperity Planner, Personal Power Kit, Tools for Transformation, Visioning Kit, even Magician's Toolkit. Now I'm back to a folder with pockets for my pages. On the front is a picture of the world taken from space, and I have written these words on the front: *I am being guided by Spirit every moment.*

Put whatever images or words you want to on the front of your folder. Call it what you will, or call it nothing at all. But, somewhere, save the work you do with this book, and continue to review it on occasion.

I am certain that single folder with the collection of dreams, plans, and other assorted things that you will write throughout this Course will be a major ingredient in your success. It is magic, in its truest, most meaningful sense — creating something out of seemingly nothing, in its own perfect time, for the highest good of all.

The complete Course, then, contains not only this book but a little book you build for yourself as well. In your own book, written in your own words, is where you'll find the most effective magic.

IF YOU ARE AN ARTIST

If you are an artist — as I was, and still am — the following words may be valuable:

You'll have difficulty succeeding as an artist — however you choose to define that success — if you ignore the world of business and refuse to be a "businessperson." Every great artist who has succeeded doing their art has been a success in business, either by taking the reins themselves and managing their own career or by working with someone else who takes those reins and takes responsibility for the success of your work. Managing an artist is not a difficult task — it is not rocket science; in fact it is much easier than creating your art.

You don't have to sell your soul to succeed as an artist. In fact, your success only expands the impact of your soul, the vision of your art, into the world.

Either you or someone close to you needs to take at least the initial steps in this Course: Clearly imagine what you want, make a simple plan to get there, and take the first steps. You don't need to do everything in this book — no one needs to do that — but you need to do *something*.

Trust your intuition; find the things in this Course that appeal to your heart and soul, and do them.

KEY 9   *Whether you choose to focus on art or business, humanitarian work or anything else, definitely write a one-page business plan. That's perhaps the single most powerful thing you can do to make the changes you want in your life.*

Make a plan, keep it short and simple, create a doable strategy for your success, and take some steps toward implementing your plan.

Don't feel you have to plan too far into the future: The plan will change over time. It will take on its own energy, and lead you to the next obvious steps to take. It may head off in an entirely different direction you can't possibly foresee at this time. That's fine. Make the plan you can make at this moment, and keep revising it as necessary.

If you don't have a good partner or manager at this time, take at least an hour or so once or twice a month and assume the role of your manager. Let your artist selves express their greatest dreams, then as your manager make a simple, clear one-page plan and do something to implement that plan — make that phone call, write that letter, talk to someone.

Be your own manager, at least until the right manager

for you comes along (and this may or may not happen; it may or may not be necessary). When you start to work with someone else as a manager, be sure to do it in a partnership way (something we go into in depth in Lessons 5 and 6), where you're still a co-manager. It's your career, after all. In your heart and in your soul you know the best career moves to make, the best way to produce and promote and distribute your work.

Above all:

> *Affirm that you can be successful*   KEY 10
> *doing what you love to do,*
> *in an easy and relaxed manner,*
> *in a healthy and positive way,*
> *in its own perfect time,*
> *for the highest good of all.*

It deserves repeating: You don't have to sell your soul to succeed as an artist. In fact, your success only expands the expression of your heart and soul into the world.

A COURSE IN BECOMING A VISIONARY

This Course gives you the tools to create a visionary business and a visionary life.

What does being a "visionary" mean to you?

To me, "visionaries" are (obviously) those who "envision," those who imagine, those who dream and, from those dreams, create possible scenarios in their imagination, their mind's eye. Every one of us has the power to imagine — and so we are all visionaries, in some way, but most of us use our powers to visualize unconsciously, and visualize only enough prosperity to barely make it. Most of us don't even dare to imagine that the quality of our lives, including our financial success and our emotional experience, could be far, far better than it is at present.

There have been many great visionaries throughout history who have led the way for us (Jesus, Buddha, Gandhi, St. Francis, Mother Teresa, and Einstein come first to mind), and there are many visionaries around today. It's good to listen to what these people have to say, and even emulate them, in some ways.

We're visualizing all the time. When you sit and think about what you want to have for lunch, you're visualizing various possibilities. You picture in some way or think about this or that possibility in your imagination, and then you decide on something and take steps to create it in reality. This is a marvelous, visionary process — something we do constantly throughout the day, though we're usually not aware of it.

We're all visionaries already, at least to some degree, so we may as well use our visionary powers to create the kind of lives we want for ourselves, and even the kind of world we want for ourselves.

This Course can show you how to be a *conscious visionary:* how to imagine what your possible success will look like, and take steps toward realizing it.

Your visionary life will probably include some kind of visionary business. Don't shy away from either word: *visionary* or *business.* There are exceptions, but most of us need to create some kind of income for ourselves, which means a business, in some form. There's no need to resist the word. After all, business can be a great force for good in the world, if used properly.

And if you think you're not a visionary, this Course will make you one. Just doing the "ideal scene" exercise, and keeping the dream of your ideal scene in mind, makes you a visionary.

THE GREAT IMPORTANCE OF REPETITION

There is repetition throughout this Course, and there is repetition of material from many of my other books, especially *Visionary Business, A Visionary Life,* and *The Ten Percent Solution* — all books I recommend you read, if you feel at all drawn to them. The repetition is intentional, for this type of material needs repetition.

> *It is only through repetition that*
> *we learn, and grow, and change.*

KEY 11

Look how many times a child repeats something new before moving on to something else. I had to hear and reflect on most of the things in this Course repeatedly before I absorbed them deeply enough to affect my life. Many of the keys in this Course are intentionally repeated, often with slightly different wording. Find a key that appeals to you and reflect on it repeatedly — and see what happens.

I have read and listened to *As You Think* by James Allen, for instance, at least fifty times, and I continue to pick it up and read it at random whenever I want a bit of inspiration. I know the two poems in the book by heart, and I quote them *repeatedly* to others, and often repeat them to myself as I'm walking or driving or just quietly reflecting.

Every time I repeat the words, it feels as if I have learned something new: I have deepened my understanding in some way, fused some new synapses, and awakened a bit more power from the universe, from the ever-mysterious depths of my powerful subconscious mind.

WORDS TO PONDER, REPEATEDLY

Here is one of the poems from *As You Think*. The other one is set in big display type at the end of this Introduction. (*"Mind is the master power that molds and makes. . . ."*) See if either one of these poems speak to you. They are filled with beautifully expressed keys to success, and to a life well lived, which is true success.

The words were written over a century ago, and are timeless, though the meanings of a few words have changed over the years: He uses "content" in the second line to mean "contentment," and uses "environment" and "circumstance" in a somewhat different way than we use them — a much broader, all-inclusive way to mean everything in our world, particularly every excuse we have ever come up with for not succeeding.

KEY 12

You will be what you will to be;
Let failure find its false content
In that poor word "environment,"
But spirit scorns it and is free.

It masters time, it conquers space,
It cows that boastful trickster, Chance,
And bids the tyrant Circumstance
Uncrown, and take a servant's place.

The human will, that force unseen,
The offspring of a deathless Soul,
Can hew a way to any goal,
Though walls of granite intervene.

Be not impatient in delay,
But wait as one who understands;

When spirit rises and commands,
The gods are ready to obey.

— James Allen, *As You Think*

When your spirit rises and you dare to dream of doing, being, and having what you want in life, the creative forces of the universe mysteriously appear and give you all the support you need.

There are no more excuses — our spirit scorns them, and is free, even able to *master time* and *conquer space.* And that is no small thing.

You have a powerful will, an offspring of a deathless soul, and it can find its way to any goal, regardless of the apparent obstacles. You have all you need within you. All resources are at your command — all you have to do is ask for them. A great visionary teacher said it all, very simply and clearly:

Ask and you will receive.   KEY 13
Seek and you will find.

— Jesus, Matthew 7:7

Mind is the master power

that molds and makes,

and we are mind, and evermore we take

the tool of thought,

and shaping what we will,

bring forth a thousand joys, a thousand ills.

We think in secret, and it comes to pass —

our world is but our looking glass.

— James Allen
As You Think

. . . .

IMAGINE YOUR IDEAL SCENE;
LIST AND AFFIRM YOUR GOALS

THIS IS THE ESSENTIAL FIRST STEP

This step is simple — all it involves is writing down a few pages of ideas — and yet it proved to be vitally important, fundamental to the rapid growth I experienced after I did it. It opened the door to every other discovery in my life, and has brought me to a level of success and fulfillment that had been completely unimaginable to me before I did this simple process.

You don't need to accept all of this as truth written in stone, and you don't need to ponder every key and master every lesson in this Course before you see results in your life. Just work with one key at a time, for as long as it feels appropriate, and that key will begin to open doors for you that will lead you to your own unique success in your own unique way.

This Course works in many different ways for different people, and on different levels within each of us at different times: Sometimes we're dealing with purely physical, material issues, sometimes mental, sometimes emotional, sometimes spiritual. We are multifaceted people, each with our own unique way of being and of doing things.

It's worth repeating: Feel free to change and adapt the material along the way. You are unique! So do it your way. Work with this material in any order and any way that appeals to you. Use these exercises to stimulate your own innate creativity. You'll end up creating a unique personalized Course that will serve to guide you in creating success as you define it to be.

A POWERFUL EXERCISE

This little exercise involves doing just a bit of writing, and then following up with the regular affirmation sessions described later. But don't underestimate this exercise because it's so simple — it will undoubtedly have a powerful and positive effect in your life, just as it had in mine.

The first step is called the "ideal scene process." It is another way to look at the second habit Stephen Covey gives us in his book *The Seven Habits of Highly Effective People.* This habit alone is a great key to success:

KEY 15

> *Begin with the end in mind.*
>
> — Stephen R. Covey
> *The Seven Habits of Highly Effective People*

This is a simple, powerful key: Begin with the end in mind, and keep the end in mind, always. Then you'll discover that the opportunities that lead you there have always been right in front of you — you just haven't seen them until now.

IS IT NECESSARY TO BE A MILLIONAIRE?

Whether your ideal scene includes being a millionaire is entirely up to you. It certainly isn't necessary for everyone, but it's a perfectly achievable goal if you feel you want that level of financial security. I know I do — and I've gone from poverty to being a millionaire using the principles and practices contained in these keys.

The important thing when imagining your ideal scene is not the money involved — the money is only a tool that helps you live the life of your dreams. A great many people can live the life they dream of without needing to become millionaires first to do it.

Being a millionaire in itself is an empty goal. What kind of life do you want to create for yourself? That's the worthwhile question to ask. What steps do you need to take in order to live the life of your dreams?

DREAM FREELY AND DEFINE SUCCESS

The important thing is to allow yourself to freely dream, and then to clearly define what success is *for you.*

The "ideal scene" exercise that follows is wonderful for giving you an easy, playful way to clearly imagine what success is for you as the unique individual you are.

Before we get to writing down our ideal scene, though, let's first reflect a bit on the meaning of success and the value of money. Some unknown writer put it this way — giving us another great key to success.

> *To live your life in your own way,*   KEY 16
> *To reach the goals you've set for yourself,*
> *To be the person you want to be — that is success.*
>
> — **Anonymous**

You may very well discover you don't need to be a millionaire at all before you can be the person you want to be. In fact, you will probably discover that being a millionaire has nothing to do with it. Having a lot of stuff, including a big house and a hefty bank account, will not make you happy or fulfilled — and has nothing to do with the person you really want to be, ultimately. (You may not agree with me at this point, and that's fine. Go ahead and get the big house and big bank account — they're perfectly wonderful goals — and once you get them you'll discover for yourself that it doesn't make you happy or fulfilled. And then you can go on to what's really important in your life.)

Don't get me wrong: Being a millionaire is a great goal, and it has the wonderful advantage of being a very concrete, achievable number. I set that goal for myself, and attained it. But I found along the way it has nothing to do with the person I want to be and the life I want to live. It has nothing to do with my happiness or deep, lasting satisfaction or fulfillment — nothing to do, in short, with what is important in life.

Understanding that makes things a lot easier for us: We don't need to achieve our goals of success in the world before we can find enjoyment and even fulfillment in our lives, because enjoyment and fulfillment are found within us, not out there in the world, and certainly not in a big house or hefty bank account or diversified investment portfolio.

As Eckhart Tolle puts it, all we need to do is get the inside right, and then the outside will take care of itself.*

---

* If all this sounds impossibly vague or confusing, I highly recommend reading or listening to *The Power of Now* or *Practicing the Power of Now* by Eckhart Tolle. Those books simplified and improved my life. If the books don't work for you, listen to his CDs titled *Living the Liberated Life* and *The Realization of Being,* or the audios on his website, WWW.ECKHARTTOLLE.COM.

THE RIGHT ATTITUDE TOWARD MONEY

In a newspaper interview, Eckhart Tolle — author of *The Power of Now* — showed us in his open and unassuming way a simple way to deal with the whole issue of money in our lives. He was asked what was it like to suddenly be so successful financially, and he said, "For years I had no money, and that was okay, and now I have money, and that's okay too."

That pretty well sums it up, doesn't it? It does no good to be frustrated about money: It is what it is, you either have it or you don't, and either way it's okay. Life goes on.

We shouldn't crave money; it will not bring us happiness. We shouldn't worship money; it is a very good servant, but a very bad master.

We shouldn't despise money, for it is neither good nor bad in itself. We need not be puzzled by money, for it is but a tool for us to use as we will, and the rules governing it are not complex, as we will see as we continue with this Course.

Here's a powerful key, an affirmation:

In an easy and relaxed manner,   KEY 17
in a healthy and positive way,
all the money I want and need is now coming to me,
in its own perfect time,
for the highest good of all.

You can substitute *abundance* for *money,* if you wish. Or *prosperity.* Or you can say a shorter form of it — something like, *Money comes to me easily as I do what I love.* Or, *My life is filled with abundance as I do what I love.*

You might want to reflect on what you've read so far before you go on to the next section. Perhaps ask yourself these questions, and just notice what pops into your head. Think about your answers for a while; play with different possibilities.

- What does it mean to you to live your life in your own way?
- What goals have you set for yourself? Are they written down? Do you remind yourself of them frequently?
- What kind of person do you want to be, ultimately?

Now we're ready to take the first step, the one that makes us visionaries.

IMAGINE YOUR IDEAL SCENE

It all starts with a dream. The essential first step is to dream and to imagine:

KEY 18

Imagine five years have passed,
and you are living your ideal life:
doing what you want to do,
being who you want to be,
having what you want to have.

Some of us don't even allow ourselves to dream — and yet it is the essential first step. Without the dream, achievement is impossible.

Take a bit of time to quietly relax, and then allow your imagination to wander. Allow yourself to dream. Encourage yourself, the way you would encourage a child, to play with different possibilities that could await you in life — if you but dare to dream.

Imagine you've been so inspired by the words and exercises in this Course — and by many other things you've encountered along the way — that you have created the life of your dreams. You have become a success in every way you

. . . .

wish. And best of all (as we will affirm later, repeatedly), you're doing it *in an easy and relaxed manner, in a healthy and positive way, in its own perfect time, for the highest good of all.*

If money were no object, and you could do, be, and have exactly what you wanted, what would it be?

WHAT ARE YOU DOING, IDEALLY?
- What kind of work and career do you have?
- What is a typical day for you?
- What do you do for relaxation and inspiration?
- What are you doing to contribute to a better world?

WHAT DO YOU HAVE?
- What have you accomplished?
- Where do you live?
- What does your home look like?
- What are your most intimate relationships like?
- What is your family life like?

WHAT KIND OF PERSON ARE YOU?
- What is the quality of your life like?
- How would someone close to you describe you?
- What are your physical and emotional states?
- What are your mental and spiritual states?

Here's where you begin to create your own version of this Course: Take a piece of paper and write "Ideal Scene" at the top, then write whatever comes to mind.

Use these questions as a starting point. Describe your *ideal*. Let it be as far-fetched as you want — we'll deal with reality later. For now, let your imagination soar. Don't restrict yourself, and don't edit it as you write it — no one else has to see it, and you can always change it later.

. . . .

We are limited only by our own imagination.

When you're finished, put your ideal scene in its own folder or notebook, or even a three-ring binder (I use a simple folder with pockets on the inside). This is the first step in creating the exact kind of life that you want, the life you've described on that sheet of paper. You are on your way to building the architecture of your success.

Don't forget this key as you do this little exercise — it was something I heard from my cousin, Katherine Dieter. She was on a yacht with a very wealthy man, and she asked him what would be the best piece of advice he could give her. He immediately said:

Don't dream too small.

That's great advice for every one of us, especially for artists, politicians, businesspeople, and those working to improve the world in some way.

LIST AND AFFIRM YOUR GOALS

When you take this next step you will see powerful results. Within your ideal scene are bound to be several different goals. Take a clean sheet of paper, write "Goals" at the top, and list your major goals, however many there are, on the page. I had ten or twelve goals when I first did my list; now I have just six — my life has gotten simpler over the years.

State your goals simply at first — maybe you'll have something like this:

- Succeeding by doing my art
- Home in the country
- $_____ in liquid assets
- A happy, fulfilling family and personal life
- Building my business successfully

AFFIRM YOUR GOALS

First we simply list our goals, in any way that comes to mind. Then we go back and rewrite each goal as an *affirmation:* words that affirm those goals are now in the process of being realized. The trick is to state your goals *in the present,* and yet put them in a way that is believable to you at present, so your subconscious mind can get to work on them.

Rewrite your goals in a way that affirms that those goals are in the process of being created now, rather than in some distant future. For the goals we listed above, rewrite them something like this:

- *I am now succeeding by doing my art.*
- *I am now finding a beautiful home in a quiet area I can easily afford.*
- *I am now building over $_____ in liquid assets.*
- *I now have a happy and fulfilling family life and personal life.*
- *My business is now growing and building, profitably and successfully.*

The most effective affirmations are stated in the present tense, and yet are entirely believable to you. They are worded so your goal is now in the process of happening — *not* that it has already been achieved, which is not believable.

I am now a millionaire is stated in the present, yet it is something your conscious and subconscious mind will have difficulty believing if, in reality, you are scrounging to pay the rent every month. Here is the affirmation that worked for me:

KEY 21

I am now creating total financial success,
in an easy and relaxed manner,
in a healthy and positive way.

As I repeated these words, I got a clearer and clearer picture of exactly what "total financial success" meant to me. It meant having the freedom to do what I want with my time. It included being a millionaire; it also included saving well over 10 percent of my income and giving away well over 10 percent — a great key we will discuss later.

As I repeated these words, something magical happened, in due time: All kinds of opportunities appeared, all kinds of possible ways to achieve the lofty goal of financial freedom started to become obvious to me, and then plans just naturally began to form in my mind. That led instinctively to the next step: making a simple, written plan for each major goal. (We'll get to that in Lesson 2.)

Once I started affirming my list of goals, I naturally over time developed clearer and clearer pictures of each of those goals — and those pictures started to include some very specific steps to take.

A FEW EXAMPLES

Not long after I started affirming *I am now finding a beautiful home in a quiet area I can easily afford,* a doable, detailed plan became clear to me: First, I would need to get into some kind of funky little starter house, anything at all to quit paying rent and start building equity. Then, after several years, the equity in that house would be enough to make the down payment on a much nicer house in a quieter neighborhood. Then — if I wanted — the equity on that house could eventually be enough to get my dream house on a hill.

That plan is exactly what happened.

Here's another example: Once I started affirming *I am now creating total financial success, in an easy and relaxed manner, in a healthy and positive way,* a detailed way to measure my success came to mind: I saw that, for me, there were four levels of being a millionaire, and I wouldn't have achieved total financial success until I had reached the fourth level.

This is the way I chose to look at it; you of course can look at it differently — and you probably will. What is true for me is not at all necessary for everyone; I'm presenting it here as an example of the kind of plans that naturally come to mind once you start affirming something. This is the plan that emerged for me. I imagined I would move through these four stages:

1. Net worth of over $1 million. (Net worth is adding up all your assets — cash, real estate, investments, art, value of personal business, etc. — and subtracting your liabilities — mortgage on home, credit-card and all other debt and loan obligations.)

2. Net worth of over $1 million, not counting the value of my business. Like a great many small business owners, I was a millionaire on paper about five years after I started my business, but almost all of my equity, almost all my net worth, was tied up in the business. It took me a while to reach the goal of having over $1 million in assets not counting the assets in my business.

3. Having over $1 million in liquid assets — cash, stocks, mutual funds, not counting the less liquid assets of real estate, the value of my business, or art.

4. Attaining true financial independence: Having enough assets to generate more than enough income to live on, so I can do whatever I want to do in life.

It took me about five years to reach the first stage, and roughly five more to reach the second. Then something interesting happened: I leapt to the fourth stage before reaching the third, for my company grew to the point where it easily supports me, and I work only as much as I want to. I achieved financial independence, and it was not necessary for me to have $1 million in liquid assets before I was able to do exactly what I wanted to do in life.

In recent years, I've been doing this affirmation regularly: *In an easy and relaxed manner, in a healthy and positive way, our company is increasing its profits by at least ___ percent per year.*

The number I put in varies. My subconscious mind has no problem accepting that affirmation, because it has come true in reality.

WORKING WITH YOUR AFFIRMATIONS

Read your goals out loud, stating them as affirmations. Do this repeatedly, and watch what happens, first in the inner world of your mind and body, and then in the outer world of your life experience and conditions.

A book reviewer once put it beautifully: When *New Age* magazine reviewed *Creative Visualization* by Shakti Gawain — a book I highly recommend — they wrote this key phrase, and it's something I certainly feel is true of this book as well as *Creative Visualization:*

* *

An open mind and heart,   KEY 22
plus the desire to greatly enrich one's life
are all you need to bring to this book —
then prepare yourself for some truly marvelous results.

Read your affirmations repeatedly over a period of weeks, and suddenly things start to happen: Ideas come to you, plans form, opportunities appear, the right people who can help and support your dreams walk into your life.

I discovered the power of imagining my ideal scene on the day I turned thirty (that birthday still remains one of the worst and one of the best days I ever had). I wrote my ideal scene down, and then made a list of the goals that were embedded in it. Over the years, there have been as many as ten or twelve of them, and as few as five or six. I wrote them as affirmations, to the best of my ability at the time, and read them nearly every morning. Then I added something we've seen before (and will see again), something I read years ago in a book by Catherine Ponder, a Unity Church minister:

Begin (or end) each goal with these words:

In an easy and relaxed manner,   KEY 23
in a healthy and positive way,
In its own perfect time,
for the highest good of all.

— **Catherine Ponder**
The Dynamic Laws of Prosperity

At times that feel appropriate, you can just say the first two lines; at other times, say all four lines, either before or after your goal.

Then say your goal to yourself, silently or out loud. Soon

you'll remember it, consciously, and before too long it will become imprinted in your powerful, creative subconscious mind.

You notice some inner changes first. They may be small, like a new idea, a new possibility that pops into your mind, or an unexpected new bit of confidence in what had been a stressful situation — or they may be major, like a great dream that unfolds in front of you in remarkable detail, a great idea, a great challenge, or a great purpose that reveals itself to you.

And once it is revealed, the first steps to take become obvious. As you take those steps, your world — in a large number of unexpected and creative ways — supports your dream. Then the next step to take becomes clear — and you take it in an easy and relaxed manner, in a healthy and positive way.

THE POWER OF IMPRINTING

The process works. My theory is that the repetition of your goals and dreams imprints them on your subconscious mind, the deep, vast part of your mind that is intimately connected with, and — in some mysterious way — united with the whole universe. By simply repeating your goals, you are aligning yourself with the creative power of the universe.

Some wise person (I don't remember who) said,

KEY 24

> *Your subconscious mind*
> *always says yes.*

That key phrase led me to another great key:

KEY 25

> *Your subconscious mind is a vast reservoir of energy*
> *that powerfully supports you in whatever*
> *you think or dream about.*

We fantasize something, we come up with a dream, and our subconscious mind says, *"Yes!"* and immediately gets to work to manifest that dream. But then so often our doubts and fears arise, and we say to ourselves, "But it's so hard to really live that dream. So few people have achieved that dream." And our subconscious mind says, *"Yes, it's so hard,"* and immediately gets to work showing us how hard it is, and the road ahead seems filled with obstacles.

Our subconscious mind is, in some ways, like a five-year-old child — though an incredibly powerful child. We have to program it with simple phrases a five-year-old can understand; we have to carefully and consciously imprint our dreams on our subconscious mind. Then the magic happens.

When we affirm we're going to create our dream, in an easy and relaxed manner, in a healthy and positive way, our subconscious mind gets immediately to work on it.

THE UNIVERSE SAYS YES

There is a powerful book I highly recommend called *The Architecture of All Abundance* by Lenedra J. Carroll. She says that it's not just our subconscious mind that says yes all the time, it is the entire universe as well. (This should have been obvious to me before, because I know our subconscious mind and the universe are inextricably linked, but it wasn't until I read Lenedra Carroll that I understood it in a new, deep-seated way that affected my life.)

Here's a great key from *The Architecture of All Abundance:*

The universe is constantly saying yes to us, yes.   KEY 26
It is our task to discover what within us
it is saying yes to....
We live in a vast and supremely responsive universe.
Within this great being, we are infinitely prosperous.

Reflect on this key awhile — can you understand this secret of success? The universe is constantly saying yes to us, constantly supporting whatever we say and think and do. What are we telling ourselves that it is saying yes to? Are we telling ourselves we are on our way to success as we choose to define it, or are we telling ourselves that life is a struggle, and maybe we don't have what it takes to succeed, or don't deserve to succeed?

The universe is supremely responsive to every thought, every word. And it is infinitely prosperous — ready, willing, and able to share its infinite abundance with you and with everyone else who asks for it.

If you can relate to these words, they can be important keys to success.

TWO POWERFUL, ALL-INCLUSIVE AFFIRMATIONS

There are two great affirmations to include in your affirmation sessions, or to say at any time during the day if you find yourself thinking or saying anything limited or destructive. The power of these words becomes obvious when you affirm them to yourself.

The first is from a famous French pharmacist, Emile Coué, who saw healing after healing in his customers after he began giving them this affirmation instead of drugs (there is more about this in *How to Think like a Millionaire*):

KEY 27

Every day, in every way,
I am getting better and better.

And when you're affirming a particular goal, it's very good to add the words that follow as a kind of "cosmic insurance policy," ensuring it will be for your highest good as well as that of others:

> *This, or something better, is now manifesting*   KEY 28
> *in totally satisfying and harmonious ways,*
> *for the highest good of all.*

Affirm it to be, and it will be. Discover for yourself the power of affirmation.

Write your list of goals, word them in the form of affirmations, and read them over repeatedly. Add your list of goals to your folder or binder, along with your idea scene.

You are creating the foundation of your success.

> *You will be what you will to be.*   KEY 29

SUMMARY

- A powerful step to take to create success — in any way you want to define it — is to imagine your ideal scene: your life and your world as you want it to be five years from now. Put it in writing, save it, and review it occasionally.
- Within your ideal scene is a list of goals. List them on a separate sheet of paper, and put it with your ideal scene.
- Each one of these goals can be expressed as an affirmation, stated in the present as if you are now already moving toward that goal. Write each of your goals as an affirmation.
- Get a separate binder of some kind (I use just a folder with pockets on the inside, or sometimes a file folder)

and put in the written exercises you do as you work with this book. Eventually, you'll create your own personalized version of this Course. It could become the most powerful key you have.

- Read your list of affirmations often, preferably nearly every day. Add these words before or after each goal: *in an easy and relaxed manner, in a healthy and positive way.* At times where it feels appropriate, also add: *in its own perfect time, for the highest good of all.*

- Your subconscious mind says yes to your dreams, goals, and affirmations, just as it says yes to every thought you have.

- Prepare yourself for some truly marvelous results!

You will become as great

as your dominant aspiration.

If you cherish a vision,

a lofty ideal in your heart,

you will realize it.

— James Allen
As You Think

. . . .

WRITE YOUR PLAN AS A SIMPLE, CLEAR VISUALIZATION

THIS KEY IS YOUR BLUEPRINT

To build anything, you need a design, a blueprint. What is your plan? To use Lenedra J. Carroll's great phrase, what is the *architecture of your abundance?*

If you've done the exercises in the previous chapter, you have a list of goals. If you're like me, you'll have two or three major goals at any given time. Now we're ready for the next step — it's another one of those keys that seems so simple and obvious that you would think more people would be doing it:

> *For every major goal,*   KEY 31
> *write a short, simple plan.*
> *Summarize it clearly on one page.*

So many people never discover this key, and think that writing a plan means creating a forty-page document with five-year projections of income and expenses and cash flow. A detailed business plan is useful if you need to raise money from certain sources (venture capitalists, banks), but most often, a plan that lengthy isn't necessary at all.

KEEP IT SIMPLE, KEEP IT SHORT

Whether you write it for a business or a personal goal, a plan is a powerful tool for *your* use. The single most important thing your written plan does is remind your powerful subconscious mind that you desire this, and you are focusing that desire by putting it in concrete words on paper so your subconscious can get to work on it.

Keep it simple: The simpler it is, the more powerfully it impacts your subconscious mind. Remember:

KEY 32
*Your subconscious mind says yes
to every one of your intentions,
and summons the forces to create them in reality.*

YOUR PLAN IS A MAP OF YOUR FUTURE

Write a short, one-page plan for each one of the major goals on your list. Perhaps you'll ultimately write a longer and more detailed plan, or the one-page version may be enough as is.

I recommend you first write the plan in your own way, without imposing any kind of structure on it. Once you've done that, you can consider possibly using some or all of the simple types of architecture I'll suggest later. But first, write your own plan in your own words — whatever words come to mind. Let your subconscious mind show you what it wants as you write that one, single page. Keep it simple:

You must simplify.
You must make the complex simple,
and then make it work.

KEY 33

— I. M. Pei, Architect

WRITTEN WORDS BECOME POWERFUL

You're developing a powerful set of written tools that will show you how to create the success you desire.

It bears repetition: If you have worked through the first lesson in this Course, you have begun to create a map to your success. You have, on paper, your ideal scene. Embedded in that vision of the future are numerous goals that you have listed on another page or two. You've rewritten your goals in the form of affirmations.

Maybe you've done it differently than this, but in some way or other you're visualizing your ideal scene. Now add a single-page plan for every one of your major goals, written in your own words.

Take this next step and, in its own perfect time, great results will happen in your life, for the highest good of all.

WRITING A ONE-PAGE PLAN

Take a sheet of paper, and write something at the top like "Plan for _____." Write your goal, big and bold, and then write in your own words a plan to reach your goal. See if you can do it on just one page — though it's fine to run longer than that, if that's what you're moved to do. Be flexible, with any and all of this material. Trust your instincts; feel free to break any rules I may seem to be providing.

Sometimes the very best plans are simply written in the

words that come up without having any structure or outline to follow. Just write your plan, in one page.

KEY 34

A one-page plan is powerful,
because it sets your powerful subconscious mind
in motion.

Once you've written it, you may want to add something based on the following outline, or even rewrite your plan using one of these two possible outlines:

A SIMPLE OUTLINE FOR A ONE-PAGE PLAN

- MISSION: Your broadest, highest reasons for doing it in the first place.
- GOALS: The steps you intend to take to fulfill your mission.
- STRATEGIES: The steps you will take to reach your goals.

In his book, *The One Page Business Plan*, Jim Horan suggests this format and defines his terms in this way:

THE OUTLINE FROM THE ONE PAGE BUSINESS PLAN*

- VISION: How do you visualize your company in the future? Where are you going with it? What will it look like in five years? Describe your idea in a manner that captures the passion of the idea.

---

* From *The One Page Business Plan* by Jim Horan (see Recommended Resources).

- MISSION: Why are you in this business? What's your passion? Why will customers buy this product or service?
- OBJECTIVES: What are the goals? What accomplishments must you achieve to be successful? List your goals in specific terms, with targets and time frames.
- STRATEGIES: What has made your business successful to date? What will make it successful over time?
- PLANS: What specific projects and actions will be taken this year to achieve the objectives?

You may have to write very small to get this on one page — two pages is fine, too.

TURNING DESIRES INTO INTENTIONS

It's worth reviewing: When you make a plan on paper, you are sending a clear message to your subconscious, and to the whole universe, and everyone in it: You have a dream or desire for something — and it has now become an *intention*. You have thought this through; you have put it on paper. You are serious; you're going to make it happen, one way or another. You intend on doing, being, or having this, in your own way — and *in an easy and relaxed manner, in a healthy and positive way, in its own perfect time, for the highest good of all.*

As soon as you intend something, the universe says yes. And it starts throwing ideas at you: You could start here; you could start there. You could do it this way, you could do it that way. Many of my plans develop their own multi-pronged strategies: First we try this, then that, and if those don't work, we go on to another possibility. Sooner or later, something starts working. Sooner or later, we reach that goal, in its own perfect time.

As soon as you intend something, you start to see opportunities where before you saw only problems and obstacles. You realize there are opportunities everywhere, always, and sometimes you see them and sometimes you don't.

There's a fascinating principle at work here:

KEY 35

What we think about expands.

If our thoughts are focused primarily on our problems and obstacles and shortcomings, those things expand and become even greater. The more we turn our thoughts to what we want to do, be, and have in our lives, the more we let ourselves imagine living the life of our dreams, the more those things expand in our lives.

Once your intention becomes solid, solutions to problems become obvious — or else what were formerly problems simply don't matter any more, and become irrelevant. Obstacles dissolve, or else you find an easier, simpler way around them.

KEY 36

In the simple act of writing a one-page plan, the architecture of your abundance is revealed to you.

A MORE EXTENSIVE BUSINESS PLAN

At times you may need a more extensive plan. If you want to raise money from investors, a longer plan is usually necessary. For whatever reasons, it'll become obvious when you need to write a longer plan.

Writing a longer plan is a powerful visualization process: If you thoroughly think it through and can make it work on paper, then you can make it work in reality.

As Jim Horan writes in *The One Page Business Plan,* "A business plan gives owners a way to test their ideas without having to put their cash or business at risk."

Feel free to skip or quickly skim over the next section, of course, if it's not necessary for you at the moment. Maybe you'll never have to do a plan longer than one page; I've only written one lengthy business plan in my whole career — and it raised the capital that launched New World Library.

CONTENTS

Begin with a Contents page — or, if you wish, the contents page can be placed after the one-page summary. Here is a sample contents page from a good, solid business plan.

CONTENTS

Income and Expense

Cash Flow

Sales Budget

Pro Forma Income and Expense

Pro Forma Balance Sheet

Appendix A — Resumes and Bios

Appendix B — Customer Responses

Appendix C — (Various supporting materials: see notes on page 49)

I — SUMMARY

BEGIN YOUR PLAN WITH A ONE-PAGE SUMMARY. This is for your own good as well as the investors'. Putting it all on one page focuses your mind, brings clarity, and — as we have seen — engages your powerful subconscious mind in the process.

In one page, state who you are, what you're going to do, and what the results will be — including, if you're bringing in investors, the form of the investment (we'll get to that next), and possibly even what a reasonable projected return on their investment could be.

II — THE COMPANY, PAST AND PRESENT

DESCRIBE YOUR COMPANY. Be brief, though it can run to several pages if necessary. Highlight the important points in bold, so people can skim through and get the gist of it. Or use this striking format: print the plan on just the right-hand pages, and have the highlights in bigger bold type on the left-hand pages. That makes it easy for anyone (including you) to quickly summarize your plan.

III — THE PRODUCTS AND/OR SERVICES

KEEP IT SIMPLE FOR THOSE UNFAMILIAR WITH YOUR INDUSTRY. Don't laden your plan with technical terms known only to those in the business. What exactly is your product and/or service? Put it in terms that someone completely unfamiliar with the industry can understand. Are you unique in some ways? Do you have a special niche?

The single biggest failing of most business plans is that the exact nature of the business — including how the money will be invested and how it will grow and be returned to investors — is not made crystal clear to investors. And there's an old saying that contains great advice: If you aren't sure what you're investing in, don't invest.

IV — MARKETING

WHAT ARE YOUR STRATEGIES? Do you have a multi-pronged marketing strategy? Spell that out first, then have additional headings for Research and Development, The Sales Process, The Distribution Network, Publicity and Promotion, and anything else important to your marketing efforts.

V — THE TEAM

EVERY SUCCESSFUL BUSINESS IS A TEAM, working together toward the same goals. List the people, and what they do, under these headings: The Management Team, The Supporting Team, and Supporting Professionals. In the last, list the people outside your company you work with regularly, including a CPA, if you have one, and agents, artists, public relations or advertising firms, and even advisors or board members.

Show that you have developed creative partnerships with all these different, resourceful people.

VI — THE FUTURE

LET YOURSELF SOAR HERE. This is the last prose section of your plan, before you get to the lists of numbers. I like to present two sets of projections here: one that is realistic and attainable, on the conservative side, and another that is optimistic but thoroughly possible. Paint your picture of what the company will be in the future. What do you realistically expect to achieve in five years — and what is your ideal scene?

VII —   THE FINANCIALS

GET OUT YOUR SPREADSHEETS. All of these may not be necessary for your particular situation, but the only lengthy plan I ever wrote had all of these reports and projections:

- SALES, EXPENSES, AND PROFITS: If your company has a history, briefly summarize the sales, expenses, and profits for the past two or three years.
- BALANCE SHEET: Your current assets minus your current liabilities.
- INCOME AND EXPENSE STATEMENT for the past six months or past year.
- CASH FLOW PROJECTIONS: A month-by-month projection for the coming year, showing cash in, cash out, and cash balance for each month. Sometimes, all you need for your plan is one year. Other times, you might need up to five years of projections, the

first two years month-by-month, the last three years quarterly.

- SALES BUDGET: Project, quarterly for the forthcoming year, your Sales, Operating Budget, Selling Expense, and General and Administrative Expense to get the Projected Profit (before taxes).
- PRO FORMA INCOME AND EXPENSE: Projections for the coming year of income minus expenses to get net profits.
- PRO FORMA BALANCE SHEET: Your projected assets and liabilities in six months, and in one year.

APPENDIXES

Here is where you can add any supporting material, including bios and resumes of key management people, responses and endorsements from customers, articles in the print media about your company, or about your industry in general — anything that would interest or educate investors or that you find worthwhile to include in your plan.

> *Whatever you can do, or dream you can, begin it.*   KEY 37
> *Boldness has genius, power, and magic in it.*
>
> — **Goethe**

FINANCING YOUR BUSINESS

If you wish to raise money with your plan, the type of investment you're looking for needs to be clearly and concisely spelled out on the opening Summary page.

There are endless creative ways to finance a company, whether it has been around awhile or is brand new. The key to successful financing is to create a win-win arrangement that works for you, your investors, and your company. (Once again, just skim or skip this section if it's not relevant at the moment.)

Remember, there are certain standards in every industry, and there are good reasons for those standards, but there are no hard and fast rules — *everything is negotiable.* Keep negotiating until you find something that works for everyone involved.

In this and in all other areas of your business (and life), use the "partnership model" as your guide, and avoid any old "dominator model" words and actions. This is quite possibly the most important key to successful business, and a fulfilling life as well:

KEY 38   *Be a partner rather than a dominator.*

We'll go into this in depth in Lessons 5 and 6 (and Riane Eisler goes into this brilliantly in *The Power of Partnership,* a book I highly recommend).

BASICS OF FINANCING

There are two basic ways to finance a company or artistic enterprise: loans and equity investments. A loan is just an agreement to pay back the money, with interest, over time. Giving equity (ownership in the company or product) can take many forms, from simple profit sharing agreements to owning percentages of the company or shares of stock. The type of equity depends on the wants and needs of the people involved, and on the structure of the business — whether it's a simple proprietorship, a partnership, a limited partnership, or a corporation.

WAYS TO FINANCE YOUR BUSINESS

There are countless ways to finance your business. The more you learn about it, the more variations and other creative possibilities there are. Look around you, talk to people, and get creative. Here are a few of the most common ways to finance a business or artistic enterprise (over the years I have used the first seven of these):

- "SWEAT EQUITY": This is how I built my business initially. I got a job in another company, saved as much as I could to put into my start-up business, and worked for my start-up (while still working for the other company) without paying myself. You build equity through your own sweat this way, and give away none of the company. This is a great possibility to consider; it leaves you fully in control of your company, with no investors to report to and to pay back.

- LOCAL "ANGELS": Once you have created a plan, make several copies and pass it around to friends and relatives. Very often, one of them will be interested in investing, or know someone else who's interested. Individuals who invest on their own are called angels, a term I've always loved. Angels are everywhere. There are angels near you! Many of them are great mentors, as well.

They need to see a clear, concrete plan. Once you write your plan, as long as you're persistent, you will find the financing you need. The key was expressed in the movie, *Field of Dreams:*

Build it and they will come.   KEY 39

- LOANS OR EQUITY INVESTMENTS FROM FRIENDS AND FAMILY: When we first started New World Library, a friend loaned us a good chunk of cash, which we repaid monthly over five years at 10 percent interest. It was a win-win arrangement. A few other friends and relatives over the first few years wanted to invest and get equity in the company, and so they became stockholders when we incorporated.

  Over the years, we bought these stockholders out when we were able to negotiate a price that felt fair to them and to the company as well.

- CREDIT CARDS: Literally millions of small businesses have been started with credit cards. You have to be careful with them; they're loans at a fairly high interest rate. But they can be wisely used, at times, when invested to make your business grow. Use them only when you have a clear plan of how you're going to pay them off, and shop around for the lowest interest rate possible.

- SMALL BUSINESS ADMINISTRATION (SBA) LOANS: This is a wonderful resource. Our first major loan was through the SBA (we found an "angel" named Bernie who connected small businesses with the SBA). For most SBA loans, you need to have at least a two-year track record as a functioning business.

  Later on, we bought our building through an SBA loan, as well. They help small businesses get commercial real estate loans; the government makes it advantageous for the banks involved as well (they get a tax break on the interest they earn).

- LIMITED PARTNERSHIPS: You can finance a wide range of businesses the way films and Broadway plays are financed. Typically, investors put up the money for a specific project or line of products, and they split profits 50–50 with those who create the product or project. We financed specific book and music projects this way in our early years — it's a great tool for artists and other creative types. A simple written agreement is all that is necessary. Consult an attorney — and tell your attorney to keep it simple.

- LIMITED LIABILITY CORPORATIONS (LLCS): This combines the advantages of a partnership with the protection of a corporation. It needs the aid of a professional in the field to set it up, as do the rest in this list. But an LLC is fairly simple and relatively inexpensive to set up.

- SMALL COMPANY OFFERING REGISTRATION (SCOR): With this nifty vehicle, you can raise up to $1 million; you file with the state. You create a stock offering that is smaller and simpler than the usual public stock offering.

- DIRECT PUBLIC OFFERINGS (DPOS): It is now much easier to offer stock to the public on a small scale than it used to be. Your friends and customers can become stockholders. See a qualified professional for details if you want to explore this further.

There are many good professionals in the financial field who can assist you in financing your business. Ask around in your community for more details. I raised all the capital I needed just by networking in my community. There are many other options, as well. Keep open to the opportunities that will come your way as soon as you've written your plan!

The Internet is another great option for finding financing. Go to any major search engine, like Google, Yahoo!, MSN, or AlltheWeb.com, and type in the words "Venture capital," "Seed money," or "Business funding." It's astounding how much information is available — literally millions of leads.

KEY 40

> *Every person is the architect*
> *of their own fortune.*
>
> — Sallust (1st century B.C.E.)

ONCE YOU HAVE A PLAN

Once you have a plan, don't forget it.

If you are working through this Course, you're accumulating more and more pages in your folder — your own condensed and personalized form of the Course. Call it what you will — that single little folder is your tool kit for success, your plan for prosperity and fulfillment.

You've written your ideal scene and listed your goals. You're affirming those goals regularly or doing whatever else feels appropriate to keep those goals in your mind and heart. For each of your major goals, you've written a one-page plan. For some of the more complex goals, you may have written a longer plan.

Return to these pages often, and go over them. Keep them current with any new additions, corrections, and updates. Go over them every New Year; go over them on or near your birthday. Every time you do, you're delivering a powerful piece of programming to your subconscious mind.

HAVE A CLEAR FINANCIAL GOAL

What is your main financial goal for the next twelve months?

It's very powerful to have a clear single number in mind — something your subconscious can get to work on, and something you definitely know at year's end whether you have achieved or not.

Whether you're in business or art, always keep a number in mind for the year's income and/or profits that you're shooting for. For many years now I've had very clear sales goals in mind, and it's pretty remarkable how many times those exact numbers were reached. I got what I projected, what I asked for — no more, no less.

For the past few years, I've been asking the powers that be to increase the profits of our company by 50 percent annually, in an easy and relaxed manner, in a healthy and positive way, in its own perfect time, for the highest good of all. In the future, maybe I'll decrease that number to 20 percent annual growth, or some other number. But for now, growing our profits by 50 percent annually seems challenging, doable, and fun.

The first year I started focusing on this, affirming it nearly every morning, our profits didn't increase at all. *Nada.* They were flat. I wondered why my affirmations didn't seem to have any effect, why my prayers didn't seem to be answered. The next year, though, our profits more than doubled, increasing more than 100 percent from the previous year — and I realized my goal had been reached, though it happened in its own perfect time.

A specific numerical goal is something your subconscious mind loves to go to work on. It is simple and unambiguous. Once you create a specific goal, you'll notice your mind begin to work on different possible ways you can reach your goal.

Begin with the end in mind — and your vastly creative subconscious mind will go to work full time to show you how to get there. You will be guided, step by step, in making your plans, and in working out your plans.

IF IT FEELS OVERWHELMING

Almost any time we try something new, especially if it's something expansive, there are times when it feels like it's too much to handle. At these times, remember this great advice from Mark Twain:

KEY 41

The secret of getting ahead is getting started.
The secret of getting started is breaking your complex,
overwhelming tasks into small manageable tasks,
and then starting on the first one.

— Mark Twain

A journey of a thousand miles begins with one small step. And it is filled with small steps, every step of the way. Just take the next obvious step in front of you.

Enjoy the scenery along the way. Enjoy each step as much as possible. It is an essential part of your journey.

KEY 42

Enjoy the journey.
There is beauty and wonder in each eternal moment,
here and now.

Here's a simple way to put it: *Enjoy your life!* It's not such a difficult thing to do — every child does it. We did it for years as children. It's good to remember what every child, every animal, every plant knows: enjoy the present moment.

ANOTHER KEY

We've been very active in this Course, making plans, listing goals, affirming those goals. It's time to consider another important key to success: Counterbalance your activity with a good healthy dose of relaxation, rejuvenation, laziness, and even (yes!) wasting time.

Our lives, our world, the whole universe is an endless movement of great polarities. Winter follows summer. Night follows day. Don't forget to follow your activity with inactivity and rest. Most of us are products of a Type-A, workaholic culture. Most of us are very good with the active side of the polarity, but neglect — or at least don't fully appreciate — the part of the polarity of life that includes loafing, relaxing, recharging, meditating, and resting.

Here's a key to take to heart:

> *Don't neglect your laziness.*   KEY 43

This Course is a lazy person's guide to success, written by a lazy person. I love being lazy. There are days when I'll get up (usually quite late, between 9:00 and 11:00 A.M.), say a brief morning prayer, have a cup of coffee, and go back to bed. Often in the afternoon or early evening I lie flat on my back for half an hour, or an hour. Sometimes I fall asleep, sometimes I just deeply relax, and sometimes I have wonderful creative meditations. I find that after I allow myself to be as lazy as I want, I'm inevitably filled with the energy to go out and do something.

Embrace the laziness within you — be fully, enjoyably lazy, as much as you can. Most of us have already fully embraced the other side of that polarity: we are active, almost all the time, the result of a workaholic, Type-A educational system and work world and society in general.

We leap out of bed and immediately start doing things. Most of us can't even take a vacation without turning it into another series of places to go, things to do and see. We come home from a vacation needing time to rest and recover from the vacation! Most of us don't need to be taught to be more active, we need to be inactive more of the time.

It's a good homework project for us all: Find more time for creative loafing. And uncreative loafing. And sleeping. And doing those things that are such an enjoyable waste of time — whatever that may be for you.

Spend time doing nothing. It brings energy and focus to the times you're doing something. It brings energy and focus to accomplishing your goals. There are times to make clear goals, and times to completely let them go — not to forget them, but to recharge, revitalize, and renew. As they say in the New Thought churches and Twelve-Step programs, *"Let go and let God."*

Take breaks as you read this book. Stretch. Talk to yourself. Take a walk. Meditate. Stare at the clouds. Do nothing for a while.

Then when you're ready to move ahead, you will do it with much more energy, clarity, and effectiveness.

SUMMARY

- To build anything, you need a blueprint. What is your plan?
- For every major goal, write a short, simple business plan. Summarize it briefly on one page. Add it to your folder containing the other things you have written: your ideal scene, your list of goals.
- A one-page plan is powerful, because it turns your

desires into intentions and sets your powerful sub-conscious mind in motion.

- If you want to raise money from investors, a longer plan may be necessary. It is not that difficult to write; take it one page at a time.

- There are endless creative ways to finance a company; the keys to successful financing are (1) write a solid plan — build it and they will come — and (2) create a win-win arrangement that works for you, your investors, and your company.

- Quite possibly the most important key to successful business, and a fulfilling life as well, is to learn to live and work in partnership with others.

- Plan your work and work your plan. Have a clear goal ahead and a clear plan to achieve it.

- At the same time, don't forget the other side of life: Balance the active with the inactive. Let yourself be lazy at times. Balance your work with some loafing and quiet time. Periods of inactivity bring energy, clarity, and effectiveness to your activity.

If you advance confidently

in the direction of your dreams,

and endeavor to live the life

you have imagined,

you will meet with unexpected success.

— Henry David Thoreau

. . . .

DISCOVER YOUR VOCATION AND PURPOSE

THIS KEY SIMPLIFIES EVERYTHING

Vocation and *purpose* are powerful words. Discovering our vocation and purpose can improve our lives, quickly and extensively. Becoming aware of what those two words mean in our lives can help us cut to the essentials, to what is important, and avoid spending years of our precious lives going nowhere. It can give us a satisfaction and fulfillment in life in a way that perhaps we haven't even yet dared to imagine. These two words give us a key to our conscious evolution.

It takes only a few minutes to reflect on this key, and to write it in a brief paragraph.

The few simple questions in this part of the Course help us focus our creative minds in the right direction. The answers to these simple questions help us make the choices that build the architecture of a fulfilled life.

Each of us is different,   KEY 45
each of us has a unique purpose for living,
and each of us has unique talents and abilities
we were naturally given to accomplish that purpose.

It's the truth, and we might as well not hide from it: We all have natural gifts — we were born with them — and we are all called to express them in some way.

We all have a natural vocation and an even greater purpose in life.

VOCATION

YOUR VOCATION IS IN YOUR IDEAL SCENE

You may have to look for your vocation, or it may be obvious to you — perhaps it has been obvious all your life. It was Kent Nerburn, the great writer, who made me aware that *vocation* comes from the Latin word for *calling*, which comes from the word for *voice*. Somewhere in your ideal scene, your vocation is calling to you.

Kent Nerburn expressed it beautifully:

KEY 46

Think of work as "vocation."
It should be something that calls to you
as something you want to do,
and it should be something that gives voice to
who you are and what you want to say to the world.
It is, above all else, something that lets you love.

— **Kent Nerburn**, *Letters to My Son*

A longer version of this quote is at the end of this chapter, in big, bold display type. They are words to the wise.*

---

* Everything by Kent Nerburn is worth reading, especially *Letters to My Son, Neither Wolf nor Dog, Small Graces, Simple Truths,* and *Calm Surrender.*

PUT YOUR VOCATION IN WRITING

Think about it. Put it in writing. It might be brief, a short paragraph, or it might fill a page. Take a sheet of paper and write "My Vocation or Calling" on the top. Then write whatever comes to mind. *It is, above all else, something that lets you love.*

Add it to your collection of pages — your personal power kit, your *Millionaire Course,* your magician's tool kit, whatever you want to call it. It is one of your keys to success.

A FEW GOOD QUESTIONS

It is certainly worthwhile to ask yourself some of these questions as well:

- In what ways are you creative?
- In what ways are you unique?
- What things do you fantasize doing?
- What do you fantasize having?
- Who do you dream of being?
- Who are you envious of? (This usually indicates we have the desire — and ability — to become what they have become.)

Here are a few more things worth asking:

- Do you feel a spiritual yearning of some kind?
- Are you frustrated or anxious much of the time?
- Do you wish to be more serene, more content with life?
- When you reach the end of your life and look back on it, what is the most important thing you want to be remembered for?

- What are the most important things for you in your life today?

Within your answers are both your vocation and purpose in life. Both are always something you're passionate about — and that is a key: follow your passion. As Joseph Campbell said, in such a concise and beautiful way:

KEY 47

Follow your bliss.

— Joseph Campbell

Isn't that great advice? Work with passion. Do what you love to do.

Oprah Winfrey has emerged as one of the greatest teachers of our time; she gave us a great reminder when she said,

KEY 48

If you don't know what your passion is,
realize that one reason for your existence on earth
is to find out.

— Oprah Winfrey

PURPOSE

You have a purpose in life.

We all have a purpose in life, and it is even greater, more expansive than our vocation. Once we realize our purpose, our lives are clarified and simplified immensely.

So many people have difficulty with the word *purpose*. You might want to find some other word for it. Whatever word you use, it's good to ask yourself this question: What is your reason for being? We have these miraculous bodies, we have a life span of however many years to express something, to do something, to be somebody. What is it?

It may require some reflection. It may take some time. But it is extraordinarily valuable to consider this question. It may be the single best thing you can do in your life.

James Allen had tremendous insight here:

> *Until thought is linked with purpose*   KEY 49
> *there is no intelligent accomplishment.*
>
> — **James Allen**, *As You Think*

You have a unique purpose for living, and you have been given unique talents and abilities to accomplish that purpose. When you realize what that purpose is, it can change and simplify your life. It can help you make major decisions you may not have even considered before, and even help you take a quantum leap ahead in your evolution and fulfillment.

Your purpose is always greater than just making money, of course. If you believe your purpose is only to make money, you will not make the right decisions, and you will never be genuinely successful. You might very well make a certain amount of money, but you'll still be unfulfilled. You will never find the contentment and fulfillment and joy of life you really want, underneath it all, for those things are only available to you when you realize you have a higher purpose in life.

THE POWER OF PURPOSE

When you discover your purpose, you marshal all kinds of forces around you and within you that support you in fulfilling every goal that is aligned with your purpose.

This is a great key:

KEY 50   *When we live and work in harmony with our purpose,*
          we are taking care of the inner work,
          and the outer world unfolds easily and effortlessly,
          bringing us the fulfillment of our greatest dreams.

Our purpose is individual and private. It is sacred. It is something to ponder, even if only a little while, and put into writing. It is something to discover for ourselves, and then do our best to remember and live by. This is the only way we will ever find real satisfaction and fulfillment.

Take a sheet of paper and write "Purpose in Life" at the top. Then write whatever comes to mind. Make it as expansive as you can. It is your great work. It is a very important part of the map to success you are creating in the pages you are writing as you work through this Course.

There is nothing new in this, of course; this part of the perennial philosophy was summed up beautifully by one of India's greatest writers, Patanjali, over two thousand years ago:

KEY 51   *When you are inspired by some great purpose,*
          some extraordinary project,
          all your thoughts break their bonds.
          Your mind transcends limitations,
          your consciousness expands in every direction,
          and you find yourself in a new, great,
          and wonderful world.

Dormant forces, faculties, and talents become alive,
and you discover yourself to be a greater person by far
than you ever dreamed yourself to be.

— Patanjali, *Yoga Sutras*
ca. 250 B.C.E.

You have taken another powerful step. You are focusing your creative energies in the highest and most effective way possible. You are becoming a powerful person able to manifest your dreams.

A SIMPLE, ENJOYABLE EXERCISE

FINDING OUR VOCATION AND PURPOSE

This simple exercise can help us find our vocation and more clearly see our purpose in life. It's very similar to the ideal scene exercise we did before, when we asked ourselves what we would do if money were no object. This time make it more specific:

Imagine you just won the lottery. Imagine suddenly having millions and millions, all the money you could ever want or need. Now answer these questions:

What would you do with the money?

What kind of life would you have?

What kind of person would you be?

Now affirm something like this: KEY 52
I am now creating the life I dream of.
I am the person I dream of being,
right here, right now.

Feel free to change the affirmation to find the words that fit your unique personality and life situation. Affirm that you are now the person you would be if you had suddenly attained everything you wish for in life.

When I did this little exercise, I imagined I had just won twenty million after-tax dollars in the lottery. I'm not greedy: twenty million is all that is necessary to set up my most expansive dream (at least at this moment), and that includes giving more than half of it away. I know that, for a lot of people, *one* million would fulfill their dreams; and many others can live a dream life on a fraction of that.

I asked myself, *What would I do with the money?*

The answer came quite quickly — it was fun, exciting to imagine it: I would give half of it away to worthwhile causes and people, leaving me with $10 million. I would put $3 million into real estate, buying my dream retreats for my wife and myself; and $3 million into liquid assets, mostly stocks and mutual funds, and work with a few different money managers to earn at least 6 to 10 percent per year — a passive income of $180,000 to $300,000 per year. I would spend about a million turning my house into my fantasy environment, and over time I would spend and give away the other $3 million.

I fully imagined the life I would have then: My dream home, my retreats in my two favorite spots in the world, enough passive income so I wouldn't ever have to work.

Then I asked myself, *What do I want all that stuff for?*

It's a good question to ask. The first time I did this exercise, I answered, *"Peace and power."* The second time I answered with a phrase I had read in *The Power of Now* by Eckhart Tolle: *"Grace, ease, and lightness."*

As I thought this through, I realized I was still under the delusion that all that stuff I fantasized about would bring me a life of ease and peace — even though I knew from experience that achieving financial goals doesn't bring any kind of lasting peace at all. It brings moments of satisfaction and joy, but they quickly pass and you find you're exactly the same person with the same core problems as before. Money takes care of some of those problems, but it also creates some new problems of its own — and, essentially, your emotional experience and your life in general doesn't change one bit. This is a depressing fact for anyone who believes that money will make them happy!

When I did this little exercise, I had already achieved everything I had dreamed of in my first ideal scene. I had a successful business and a family and the big white house on the hill. I was a multimillionaire. But these things had not brought me the ease and peace that I thought they would when I dreamed them up in the first place.

So I came up with this affirmation:

> *I now have peace and power.*   KEY 53
> *I now have grace, ease, and lightness.*

Don't underestimate this little exercise. It made me realize something important:

> *Every millionaire discovers that being a millionaire*   KEY 54
> *is not the important thing in life:*
> *The important thing is to live the life you dream of living*
> *and to be the person you dream of being.*

Whether you believe it or not, money has nothing to do with any kind of lasting happiness. Perhaps you will have to make a lot of money before you truly realize this, but if you can understand it right now — regardless of your financial situation — it can save a lot of wasted time and effort.

YOU DON'T NEED TO WIN THE LOTTERY

You don't need to be a millionaire before you can be at peace, or even before you have the power to do, be, and have what you want in life. And finding what is meaningful in life has absolutely nothing to do with our bank accounts or real estate or anything else out there in the world. We can find peace and satisfaction to some degree in the outer world when we learn how to live and work in loving partnership with others, but we can find real, lasting peace only within, because that is where it is. It surpasses all our understanding; it is unchanging and eternal, forever waiting for us to discover it.

You've heard it said another way many times before:

KEY 55   *The Kingdom of Heaven is within.*

Eckhart Tolle said it clearly and simply:

KEY 56   *If you get the inside right,*
                    the outside will fall into place.
                    — Eckhart Tolle, *The Power of Now*

He went on to give us more words worth remembering:

If you are dissatisfied with what you have got, or even frustrated or angry about your present lack, that may motivate you to become rich, but even if you do make millions, you will continue to experience the inner condition of lack, and deep down you will continue to feel unfulfilled.

You may have many exciting experiences that money can buy, but they will come and go and always leave you with an empty feeling and the need for further physical or psychological gratification. You won't abide in Being* and so feel the fullness of life now that alone is true prosperity.

---

* Eckhart Tolle uses the words *Being* or *Presence* to describe the "peace that passes all understanding" that is found within. He says you could use the word God, but he prefers Being or Presence, because people don't argue about those words: No one believes their being is greater than another person's being.

FINDING YOUR PURPOSE

IS YOUR PURPOSE STILL UNCLEAR?

Many people have said to me, over the years, "I don't know what my purpose is — how can I find it?"

My advice is simple: *Ask for it.* Then listen for an answer.

You can ask no one — or nothing — in particular. Or you can ask your own intuition, your own subconscious mind. Or you can ask the creative force of the universe, in any name you choose to give it. It's a key we've seen before:

> *Ask and you will receive.*   KEY 13
> *Seek and you will find.*
>
> — Jesus, Matthew 7:7

You can pray for it. You can sit quietly or take a quiet walk somewhere, and ask, "What is my purpose, underneath it all, or above it all? Show me what it is. Tell me what it is!"

Then wait for the answer.

Be as quiet as you can and listen to any words that softly come to mind. An inner voice might speak to you immediately. Or you may have to ask the question again, and listen again, before you hear a still, small voice within. Or maybe you'll hear it an hour later, or while you're taking a walk the next day. Or you'll find your answer in a dream. Or in the remark of a friend. Or in something you hear on the radio or on TV. Or in a book or magazine. Or on the Internet. Or in a child's song. Or on a billboard. Or in a sunset, a moving stream, the flight of a hummingbird, or a cloud drifting overhead. It could come from anywhere.

Ask for it, then wait for it, and it will come.

A VISION QUEST

If the answer doesn't come after a while, take a few days off, or even a week or more. Go off, alone, to some place quiet and private. Be alone with yourself. Say your prayer every morning and every evening, asking for guidance. Throughout the day, ask your questions.

This time of retreat is immensely worthwhile, and a great purpose will emerge for you, a great mission, if you ask for it, and the perfect vocation will be a part of it.

Your life will take on new meaning, for you will have found your connection, not just to your work — your vocation — but also to your Great Work — your purpose. Life will be much simpler, easier, and more enjoyable.

PUT IT IN YOUR OWN WORDS

You are an original, and your purpose will be expressed in the perfect words for you. Here's a hint — your purpose always has something to do with growth, with expansion into new areas, with both personal and planetary evolution.

As Barbara Marx Hubbard shows us in her great book, *Conscious Evolution,* we are ever-evolving beings and have reached a stage where we can choose to consciously evolve. This is certainly part of our purpose in life.

WHEN WE DISCOVER OUR PURPOSE

A great change takes place when we first become aware of our purpose in life. Life becomes simpler. Decisions become easier.

A great healing occurs, for all the diverse aspects of our being become unified: Our physical, emotional, mental, and spiritual components become linked together, in one focused whole — and healing, magic, and miracles result.

Once we discover our spiritual nature, it infuses the mental and emotional and physical parts of our being with life, love, and creative power. When our minds, emotions, and bodies are attuned to our spirit and our purpose, they become filled with healing, creative energy. Our minds infuse our emotions and bodies with intelligence and power. Our emotions infuse our minds and bodies with love and enthusiasm and its attendant creative power.

We fully realize what it means to be alive, what it means to be, as James Allen puts it in *As You Think*, "a being of power, intelligence, and love." We discover the truth of his great words:

As a being of power, intelligence, and love,   KEY 57
you hold the key to every situation,
and contain within yourself that transforming
and regenerative agency by which you may
make yourself what you will.

— James Allen, *As You Think*

It's worth repeating: If this is a bit too metaphysical or spiritual for you, don't worry about it. Skip over anything that's not appropriate for you at this time, or change any words that may not be appropriate for you. The words themselves aren't important — it's the ideas behind them that are keys to great growth and change. Discover what these powerful ideas are *in your own words*.

ACHIEVING OUR PURPOSE

Once we fully discover our purpose, we discover the means to achieve it. It is contained within the purpose itself;

it is contained within you. Within you is your purpose and vocation; within you are the keys to the greatest fulfillment of your desires. You have only to ask what they are, and then listen.

Ralph Waldo Emerson said that we would not have our desires in the first place if we didn't also have the means to fulfill those desires. Deepak Chopra took that idea to another level:

KEY 58

Within every desire
is the seed and mechanics for its fulfillment.
— **Deepak Chopra,** *Creating Affluence*

For every significant desire you have, you can create and implement a plan for its fulfillment. If you take these keys to heart, and remember them, they can change not only your life but your whole world as well.

SUMMARY

WE HAVE NOW TAKEN THE MOST
IMPORTANT STEPS

Continuing to work with the steps and keys in the first three chapters of this book may be all you need. Let's review them. The repetition will do us good.

I discovered the first step — writing an ideal scene — on my thirtieth birthday. The next few steps came almost immediately after, over the next few days. All the other steps, or keys (call them what you will), that follow the first three lessons in this Course were things I discovered over the next ten or fifteen years, and each of them has been tremendously helpful. But I am certain it was the repetition of these first few steps that made all the difference, moving me from small-thinking poverty to expansiveness and abundance, from frustration to a deep, never-failing sense of gratitude and fulfillment.

So it's worthwhile to review these first few steps:

- WRITE YOUR IDEAL SCENE.

  This takes a lot of thought, and over time, more and more pieces of it will fall into place for you.

  Every ship needs a destination, otherwise it wanders around aimlessly and gets nowhere. What is your destination? Where do you want to go in life? Who do you want to be? *Begin with the end in mind.*

  Once we have our destination in mind, we make a plan to get there. Once we make a plan, the first step to take becomes obvious. Once we take that step, the next becomes obvious. We move forward, in an easy and relaxed manner, in a healthy and positive way — and, in its own perfect time, we arrive at our destination.

> *The human will, that force unseen,*
> *the offspring of a deathless soul,*
> *can hew its way to any goal,*
> *though walls of granite intervene.*
>
> — James Allen, *As You Think*

KEY 59

- MAKE A LIST OF GOALS.

  Within your ideal scene is every significant goal you have at the moment. List all of the major goals. There may be just a few, or you may have ten or twelve or more.

- AFFIRM YOUR GOALS.

  Rewrite your goals in the form of affirmations. Word them so that they are in the process of happening now, with words such as these: *In an easy and relaxed manner, in a healthy and positive way, I am now achieving success and fulfillment* (or) *I am now taking a quantum leap in my artistic success (or business success), in its own perfect time, for the highest good of all.*

Nearly every day, read and affirm your goals. This immediately puts your limitless subconscious mind to work.

Here's a possible affirmation — feel free, of course, to change the language to make it your own:

KEY 60
I now work and live in harmony with my purpose.
I am now doing the inner work,
and the outer world, easily and effortlessly,
is now bringing me the fulfillment of my dreams.

• MAKE A ONE-PAGE PLAN FOR EACH
  IMPORTANT GOAL.
  Word it simply, so it penetrates to your subconscious mind. You may need to make longer, more detailed plans for some of your goals, but be sure you have a clear, simple one-page plan for every major goal: a summary for you and all others involved to easily grasp.

• REFLECT ON AND WRITE YOUR VOCATION AND
  PURPOSE IN LIFE.
  Take the time to ask these essential questions, and listen for the answers:

  What is your vocation, your calling?
  What is your highest purpose in life?

When you have a vocation, your work becomes your pleasure. When your plans are aligned with your purpose, you will inevitably succeed, for you will discover opportunities everywhere and receive all kinds of support from sources you never even dreamed of when you began this adventurous journey.

You will be what you will to be. KEY 29

— James Allen, *As You Think*

Think of work as

Vocation.

It comes from the Latin word for calling,

which comes from the word for voice.

In those meanings it touches on what work

really should be.

It should be something that calls to you

as something you want to do,

and it should be something that gives voice to

who you are and what you want to say to the world.

A vocation fills you with a sense of meaning.

It is something that you choose because of

what it allows you to say with your life.

It is, above all else, something that lets you love.

— Kent Nerburn, *Letters to My Son*

LESSON 4

· ·

SEE THE FULL HALF OF THE GLASS, THE BENEFITS IN ADVERSITY, AND KEEP PICTURING SUCCESS

MOVING FROM STRUGGLE TO SUCCESS

This simple key gives us a way to clearly see the difference between those who create success and those who continually struggle — and once we see it, we can see how to move from struggle to success in our own right.

SEE THE FULL HALF OF THE GLASS

THE GREAT GIFT OF LIFE

We have all been given a great gift — the gift of life. The cup that is our life is half-full, half-empty. We choose, consciously or unconsciously, which half we focus on — and what we focus on is what we create in our lives.

This is an important key to remember, though it seems easy to forget in the course of our busy days — though if we use some of the tools in this Course, our busy days can become easy and relaxed, healthy and positive instead of stress-filled busyness.

An old friend of mine has had his own business for

years, and it has been a constant struggle. We keep meeting and talking, and I invariably end up trying to give him some of this material, some of these keys. And yet he's stuck in the same old rut, year after year, struggling to survive, scrounging to pay the bills, barely making his payroll.

He is passionately trying to do what he wants to do, though he has all kinds of conflicts about it, and a wife who wants him to do something else because he struggles so much. He works very hard — much harder than I do, probably twice as many hours per week — yet he seems unable to see where he is undermining all his efforts.

A POWERFUL IMAGE

One day I asked myself, as he was giving me his ongoing litany of problems, what is at the core of his difficulties? How can we get to the bottom of it all? And the image of the half-empty, half-full glass immediately came to mind, and then this phrase (which we've seen before): *What we think about expands.*

It's a very good thing that the image of the half-empty, half-full glass has become so well known, because within it lies a very important key to fulfillment, to realizing the life of our dreams:

KEY 62

Each one of us has been given a great gift:
the cup of life.
It is half full and half empty.
We choose which half to focus on, at every moment.

The full half contains all our unique gifts and strengths, all our dreams and creative ideas, but the empty half is a constant reminder, if we choose to focus on it, of everything

we lack: all our shortcomings, doubts, fears, problems, obstacles.

It is all part of the great polarity that is at the foundation
of our lives and our world. It is the Tao (or God, or the universe, or chemistry, or physics, or whatever you choose to call
it), with its endless interactions and continuous interplay of
light and dark, activity and stillness, *yin* and *yang*. If we didn't
have emptiness, there would be no fullness; if we had no dark-
ness, there would be no light. Each thing needs its opposite to
define it and even create it. All life is a play of these opposites,
so it's best to embrace it all — our greatest dreams and our
deepest fears, our strengths and weaknesses — and acknowledge and work and play with both sides of the polarities.

My friend was *nearly continuously* focusing on the empty
half of the glass, on what was wrong, to the point where he
almost never considered the full half, even though it is the only
place where he can find what he needs to overcome the seemingly endless problems and obstacles of the empty half.

That's the key: Spend more of your time focusing on your
fullness, your strengths, your dreams, your plans — the
things you love in life — and less time on the things that are
preventing you from realizing your dreams. *What we think
about expands.*

> *Unsuccessful people focus on the problems;*   KEY 63
> *the successful focus on the solutions.*
> *Focus on your fullness, your strengths, your dreams —*
> *the things you love in life.*

Unsuccessful people focus primarily on the difficulties,
on what isn't working. They complain a lot, or else suffer in
silence. They struggle; they are powerless. What they give
their attention to expands in their minds and in their lives.

Successful people focus primarily on what is working and what could conceivably work in the future — and, just like everyone else, what they give their attention to expands in their minds and in their lives. They focus more on possible solutions than they do on the problems. They're aware of their abilities and gifts, and even more aware of their dreams and desires, and they look at problems and obstacles as creative challenges. And so they inevitably move toward the fulfillment of their dreams. Any failures along the way are simply necessary steps they have to take to realize those dreams.

Successful people have discovered something very important:

KEY 64

When you focus on the half of the glass that is full,
when you focus on your dream
and on how it can be fulfilled,
you discover everything you need to create success.

You could put it this way: Within the half of the glass that is full is everything you need to connect to the abundant fullness of the universe.

OVERCOMING PROBLEMS AND OBSTACLES

Successful people become powerful not by denying their weaknesses and shortcomings and problems, but by fully acknowledging them. Perhaps one of the most important things I do in my seminars is show people as many of my weaknesses and shortcomings as I can. I find great joy, in fact, in telling people I'm basically lazy (I don't do mornings, for instance, or Mondays, or Sundays), I'm extremely disorganized (my desk is chaos), I'm not that smart (financial balance sheets are still a mystery to me), I have a spotty memory, I neglect to do important things, I lose things because my filing system is completely dysfunctional, I forget people's names and entire conversations, even some that are important to my business or social life — the list goes on and on.

One of the most important things I can show people is this: *Whatever* problems, obstacles, or shortcomings you have don't matter — in the long run the only thing that matters is *where you focus your attention.* This is not a theory — I have found it to be true in my life, over and over:

> **As soon as your dream becomes stronger**
> **than your doubts and fears,**
> **your dream begins to manifest.**

KEY 65

We prepare ourselves first by dreaming, and then by imagining a plan; in doing so we are simply and naturally focusing on the full half of the glass — on our gifts. Somewhere in the full half we can always find creative solutions for any problems or obstacles that arise. This process is effortless, and can show us how to live the life of our dreams, doing what we love to do in our lives.

All of us are talented, and none of us are perfect. All of us have unique strengths and abilities, and all of us have unique weaknesses and imperfections. All of us have been given the ability to shine brilliantly in some areas of life, and we are all clueless and ignorant in other areas. All of us are gifted, and we all need help.

If we had to be perfect before we could succeed in life, none of us would ever succeed.

YOU DON'T HAVE TO SEE THE ENTIRE PLAN

If we wait before we begin the projects we fantasize about until we see the entire plan of how they're going to come to fruition, we'll probably never get started. You don't have to see the entire plan — it's going to change and evolve over time anyway. All you need to do is to see the next step in front of you, and then take that step. Let the universe work out the details of the plan farther on down the road.

Keep focusing on the half of the glass that is full, and move forward in spite of any fears and doubts that come up.

NOTICE AND ACCEPT THE HALF-EMPTY SIDE

All of us have doubts and fears. All of us have problems and difficulties and conflicts. All these things need to be fully acknowledged — they are certainly not to be denied — but focusing excessively or even compulsively on the empty half of life leads to neurosis and failure.

When a problem arises from the half-empty side of life, look carefully at it, acknowledge it and express it, and then bring in all the creative fullness of the other side of life, the full side, to confront it and deal with it. Hide nothing from yourself — the good, the bad, and the ugly — but don't focus too long on the problems. Get your creative mind working on solutions instead, and those solutions will appear. (This is an ever-recurring theme throughout this Course; we go into it in depth in Lesson 10.)

SUCCESSFUL PEOPLE FOCUS ON
THE FULL HALF

When you focus on the half-full side of life, you discover something marvelous, in the fullest sense of the word: The

half-full side quickly grows fuller and fuller, and connects you
with a world of opportunities and abundance.

When you focus on your strengths, you become stronger,
more confident, more able to take risks. When you are aware
of your unique gifts, you have a good amount of healthy self-
esteem, and over time you come to believe you are capable of
creating success, as you define it, as you desire it. You come
to believe it not through making some kind of leap of faith,
but by seeing the results that actually happen in your life. You
fully realize at some point in this process that you are capable
of living the life of your dreams, regardless of your flaws,
fears, doubts, excuses, neuroses, shortcomings, poor education, lack of experience, lack of money, dysfunctional family,
etc., etc.

Keep focusing on the fullness of your life: KEY 66
Keep remembering your dreams, your strengths,
your unique talents and skills.
Be absolutely, uniquely, fully yourself
and you have everything you need
to create the life of your dreams.

GOOD QUESTIONS TO ASK

To help you become aware of which half of the glass you
tend to focus on, ask yourself these questions:

- What are the things that are keeping you from living
  the life of your dreams?
- What are all your excuses? (Here's a key to success:
  None of your excuses are valid.)
- What are all the good things you bring to the party?
- What gifts, abilities, strengths, and talents do you have?

If you tend to spend more of your energy focusing on the empty half of life, remember: As soon as you spend more time on your dreams, plans, and gifts than on doubting and complaining, success will come to you as naturally and inevitably as spring follows winter.

SEE THE BENEFITS WITHIN ADVERSITY

A LIFE-CHANGING PHRASE

Many years ago, I heard a single phrase that had a great impact on my life. I don't remember where I first heard it or read it, and for years I didn't know who first said it, but the words resonated with something in me, and I immediately wrote the phrase down:

Within every adversity is an equal or greater benefit.

As soon as I heard it, I thought, *This is important. I need to remember this.* I put it on my desk, right by the phone, where I saw it often.

At the time, I was at just about my lowest point financially; my business and life were a series of emotional struggles. That single phrase almost immediately helped shift my perspective in some critical areas of both business and life. It has opened many new doors to me that I didn't even know existed — doors to new levels of abundance and fulfillment. It has turned out to be an invaluable key to success, one of the most important of all, one I return to and use over and over.

Years after I heard it, someone told me it was from Napoleon Hill, the author of the classic book, *Think and Grow Rich,* and the exact words are "Within every adversity is the seed of an equal or greater benefit."

I later heard it phrased in another way that is just as

good: *Within our problems, within our apparent obstacles, are opportunities.*

Do you see how remembering this key in difficult situations can immediately shift your thinking from the half-empty to the half-full side of the glass? It can open the floodgates of your imagination and release a vast amount of previously undiscovered ideas, creativity, and intelligence.

> *Within every adversity*   KEY 67
> *is an equal or greater benefit.*
> *Within every problem is an opportunity.*
> *Even in the knocks of life we can find great gifts.*

I just discovered the last line of that key a few years ago in *The Bhagavad Gita,* the classic sacred work that originated in India over five thousand years ago.

When you work with these keys for a while, they become part of who you are. When your subconscious mind incorporates these messages, your life changes dramatically. You see evidence of this everywhere throughout the day, even in your dreams at night.

PAY ATTENTION TO YOUR DREAMS

Keep working with these keys, and you'll start to have some amazing dreams — if you haven't had them already!

Pay attention to your dreams as you work with this material. Your dreams will help you in this adventure; they will give you a great amount of guidance. As you go to sleep, repeat to yourself, *I will remember my dreams, and their meaning will be clear to me.* This is a great little technique that can open up the world of dreams for you, and allow you to tap into the wisdom and power of your subconscious mind.

I've had dreams that dissolved all kinds of apparent obstacles in my life, dreams that were worth years of therapy, dreams that showed me the full half of the glass of my life in brilliant detail. I've had dreams that have showed me my vocation and purpose in life. I've heard new songs in dreams. Sometimes dreams will have short little messages — sometimes profound, sometimes mundane, practical things to remember to do.

In one dream I was talking to a musician friend of mine, and I said, "You know, success in music is just 5 percent talent and 95 percent management."

That's great advice for artists of all kinds.

In another dream I had, someone came up to me and said, "Can you really get what you want in life?" A TV screen suddenly appeared in front of us, and someone on the TV said, "Not if you think like everybody else."

That's great advice for everyone.

Your dreams are important: They are messages from your subconscious mind confirming it has received its instructions and is moving you on to new levels of success, understanding, peace, and power — as much as you're ready for at this moment.

FINDING CREATIVE SOLUTIONS

In *The Architecture of All Abundance*, Lenedra J. Carroll gives us another great key: a simple exercise that can show us how to open the gates of discovery within us and find creative solutions to the problems we encounter. She calls it "the twelve *What Ifs*."

When you're confronted with a problem, first take a while and reflect on these questions: What possible benefits can there be within this problem? What opportunities? What gifts?

Then take a sheet of paper and list as many possible outcomes of the problem as you can. *What if* this happened? What if that happened? What if I did this? What if I did that? Lenedra Carroll suggests listing twelve possibilities, twelve *what ifs*.

When I first tried this, I got to just two *what ifs* — and the next time just to three — before the perfect solution appeared, and I had no need to list more. I've done it many times now; the most I've been able to list so far has been seven or eight. But every time I've done it, it has been very helpful; sometimes when I've done it, it has been a mentally and emotionally expansive experience that has led to solutions I wouldn't have dreamed of otherwise.

This is a superb exercise for discovering creative possibilities. There aren't just one or two possibilities for us in any given situation; there are at least a dozen, with an infinite number of variations within each one of them.

> *Create a list of "What ifs" for each problem*   KEY 68
> *or obstacle you face,*
> *and a great many new creative possibilities*
> *will be revealed to you.*

Keep working with these keys, and creative solutions will appear to even the greatest problems and obstacles you will ever encounter.

KEEP PICTURING SUCCESS

DREAM, IMAGINE, BELIEVE, CREATE

My wife gave me a silver picture frame, with four words inlaid into the silver, one on each side: *Dream, Imagine, Believe, Create.*

I treasure that little frame, because it sums up the whole process I keep trying to communicate to others. First you allow yourself to dream. Then you imagine different possibilities, and let some of them evolve into concrete plans. Then you start creating exactly what you've planned. Belief is a by-product of the process: As soon as you see it working, you naturally come to believe it.

This is not rocket science; it can be expressed in simple words everyone can understand.

KEY 69

The key to achieving success is to be able to clearly imagine it.

It seems so obvious, doesn't it? These principles are easy to understand — though implementing them can be challenging. Yet dealing with the challenges and obstacles that arise when we dare to dream and to act on those dreams is certainly one of the most expansive and fulfilling things we can do.

A PULL TOWARD EXPANSIVENESS

If you've ever had a peak experience, or even a moment of insight that shifted something within you, you know it's not easy to clearly describe it to others. It's the same with these keys. Some of them won't affect you in any way, but many of them will resonate with something in you that is ready for change and expansion.

We are evolving beings; it's in our genetic code. When we do the same repetitive activity over and over, we become bored, and we naturally start to look for new challenges. A friend of mine quit his well-paying job simply because he was no longer learning anything new. He started over in an entirely new industry just so, as he put it, he could "fuse new synapses."

We want to grow; we want to learn new things; we want to be challenged in some way. A deep part of us senses that new growth is part of our great purpose in life. And yet, so many of us ignore it and resist it and settle for less than we're capable of — why?

There are many different reasons: maybe we feel we need security, or a regular paycheck, or we have obligations to others, or we don't have enough self-confidence, or we're afraid of failure, or we think we need more time, talent, or money than we have — the list goes on and on and on.

But the bottom line might be this: *We failed to dream, or have forgotten our dream.* And so we settle for so much less than we could have attained.

Henry David Thoreau wrote, "Most people live lives of quiet desperation." That was putting it bluntly, even harshly. I prefer the way Martha Graham, the great dancer and choreographer, expressed it: "We are driven by a divine discontent." We feel a pull toward expansiveness, a desire for something greater. If we don't do something about it — take even a few small, tentative steps forward — we will remain unfulfilled.

Where do we start?

With a dream.

What do you dream of doing, being, having?

What kind of life and what kind of work do you feel pulled toward?

We start by daring to dream, and daring to make a plan to accomplish that dream — and then suddenly the steps become obvious, and we discover we have everything we need to take those steps and implement that plan. We discover this powerful key:

We're surrounded by opportunities, always.
We see them as soon as we begin to look for them.
We find them when we ask for them.

RESISTING THE PULL TOWARD EXPANSIVENESS

At the same time, we discover all kinds of *resistance* to our dreams — and it seems like the greater the dream is, the greater the resistance. Some of it comes from other people, but most of it comes from within us. In this Course we find ways to deal with our inner resistance (especially in Lesson 8, but all throughout the Course as well). Once we deal with our inner resistance, our outer problems have a way of shrinking to a manageable size, or even dissolving. That's why I so often repeat that almost all the work — all of the *important* work — is internal. Get the inside right, and the outside will take care of itself, easily and effortlessly, in a healthy and positive way, in its own perfect time, for the highest good of all.

You'll know you've overcome your doubts and fears when suddenly you discover you have created exactly what you were wishing for — it has magically appeared before you, in living color, in physical reality.

THE KEY TO BEING LUCKY

Now that I have attained so much, people often say I am "lucky." Why do some people seem to be lucky and others un-lucky? Somewhere along the way I heard a good explanation: Luck doesn't just happen to us, at random, for no good reason — we create our own luck when we keep picturing success and preparing for it, and taking whatever steps we can take.

Luck is preparedness meeting opportunity.   KEY 71
When you prepare,
opportunities present themselves.

The opportunities were always there, but you didn't see them before because you hadn't prepared for them. Once you prepare for them, they become obvious to you. They are everywhere.

It seems as if we have no control over the opportunities that come our way, but we can certainly start preparing for our success. There is always something we can do today or in the near future, even if it's just a small step: a simple one-page plan on paper, a bit of research, a phone call, a note in your calendar to do something.

Those who succeed have a clear,   KEY 72
focused picture of their success.
The level of success they attain matches
the expansiveness of their dreams.

DO I DESERVE SUCCESS?

Do you have a hard time picturing success because you feel, on some deep level, you may not deserve it?

This is a question most people — including me — have grappled with. *Do I deserve it?* There are lots of doubts and fears suggesting maybe I really don't deserve success. Maybe I haven't worked hard enough. I'm certainly lazier than most people seem to be. Maybe I don't have the necessary talent, energy, abilities, education, money, looks, competitive spirit, fire in the belly, emotional stability, background, luck, or *whatever* I think is necessary for success.

I wrestled with this stuff for several years, and then one

day I realized something (because of my background and up-bringing, this key came to me in religious terms, but you can state it in a completely secular way if you wish):

KEY 73   *Jesus said, "Ask and you will receive."*
He didn't say, "Ask and you will receive —
if you deserve it."

It's not a matter of *deserving* success. Don't even bother to go there. Don't even worry about whether you deserve it or not. It's a waste of time and energy because it's all based on fears and doubts that are unfounded — just as *all* our fears and doubts are, once we really get down to it.

If you can't just let it go, if you still grapple with the issue, look at it this way: We're all God's children — whatever term you want to use for it — we're all the children of an abundant universe, and we all deserve the kind of success we want to give to our own children. We all deserve to have happiness, peace, and personal fulfillment.

IS IT GOD'S WILL?

This is another question I grappled with for years. I have prayed for years to do God's will, but is it truly God's will for me to have great success? To have a mansion on a hill? Piles of gold? A well-balanced investment portfolio? Didn't Jesus live in poverty? Didn't he say it is harder for a rich man to enter the Kingdom of Heaven than for a rope to pass through the eye of a needle? (That's the correct translation, incidentally: not a camel, but a rope. Not that it matters; both are nearly impossible to get through the eye of a needle.)

I was filled with doubts that I deserved my dreams in the first place, and filled with fears that if I did somehow manage to create the stuff of my dreams, they would corrupt me and send me wandering off in a direction contrary to God's will and to a life well lived.

Then I had a child. That certainly brought major changes in my life, including a love I have never known before and some insights as well.

I asked myself what I wanted most for my child, and realized I want him to be fulfilled in any and every way that he wants to be. I want him to do, be, and have whatever he wants in life. I want him to live the life of his dreams. That is my will for my son.

And then I realized that my will for my son is exactly the same as God's will for me — and for you as well. God wants us to have exactly what we want for our children: God wants us to be fulfilled, to be fully, uniquely who we are, without limitation, for we are no less than a unique and miraculous creation of a vast and endlessly creative universe.

CELEBRATE GLORIOUS FAILURE!

I have a friend who creates magic on a stage, director and playwright John Clarke Donahue. He always comes up with something worth pondering and repeating every time I talk to him. He recently launched into something like this:

"We should celebrate glorious failure! Why be afraid of failure? Why not celebrate it? When we allow ourselves to fail — in small ways and in glorious huge flops — we're guided to great things by our creative spirit."

Celebrating failure allows us to picture success more freely. This is a great key to discovering the far reaches of our creative spirit.

Celebrate glorious failure!   KEY 74

Most successful people I know, including me, love telling stories of their failures. Our failures are the cost of our education. We learn from our mistakes. Embedded in each one is always some great lesson we needed to learn in order to succeed.

Stories of failure are great teaching tools. They can teach us what *not* to do, and that's invaluable.

KEEP YOUR EYES ON THE SUCCESSES

It helps to more clearly picture your own unfolding success story if you keep your eyes on other people's success stories as well. In whatever arena you imagine, there have been those who have succeeded brilliantly, there have been those who have failed spectacularly, and there have been those who just muddled along and barely supported themselves.

Which one of these paths do you choose?

Keep focusing on those who are successful, and you'll soon be joining them. When I first began my little company, I heard far more stories about failure than about success. I was told 80 percent of new businesses fail; I was told you can't make money in publishing.

But as I looked around, I saw some success stories, too: people who were supporting themselves very well doing what they loved, people who were making millions of dollars, even in publishing. When I look back, I can see that it was remembering and focusing on the success stories that helped me keep moving toward success.

THE KEY IN A NUTSHELL

You dream, you imagine.

You create a plan.

You create a great challenge, with many apparent obstacles.

As you encounter these difficulties, these problems, you look at each one and ask,

What is the opportunity here?

What is the benefit in this difficulty?

What is the gift?

If you keep imagining, and keep looking for the opportunities, benefits, and gifts that come to you, you will succeed, without a doubt. It is inevitable.

YOUR CONDENSED VERSION OF THE COURSE

Add any notes or quotes from this lesson and from the rest of the lessons that follow in this Course to your folder. In the first three lessons, we covered all of the essential ingredients in your folder — your ideal scene, your goals, your plan, your vocation, and your purpose. From here on throughout the Course, feel free to add anything at all you feel moved to put in your folder.

Work with it in your own creative way to make it a tool that works for you. Be sure to review the items in your folder regularly.

SUMMARY

- Each of us has been given a great gift: the gift of life. It is half full and half empty. We all have unique strengths and abilities, and we all have weaknesses, fears, and challenges.

- When you focus on the half of the glass that is full, when you focus on your dream and how it can be fulfilled, you discover everything you need to create the life of your dreams.

- All of us are talented; none of us are perfect. Fortunately we don't need to be perfect to be successful. In fact, we already have all the tools we need to be successful.

- Within every adversity is an equal or greater benefit. Within every problem is an opportunity. Even in the knocks of life we find great gifts. This is a great key to success.

- Those who succeed have a clear, focused picture of their success. The success they attain matches the expansiveness of their dreams. The key to achieving success is to be able to clearly imagine it. Once you clearly imagine it, opportunities appear all around you.

- "Luck" is preparedness meeting opportunity. When you prepare, opportunities present themselves.

- Jesus said, "Ask and you will receive." He didn't say, "Ask and you will receive, if you deserve it." It's not a matter of whether or not you deserve it, or whether or not you even need it: Simply ask for it, and then prepare to receive it.

- Celebrate glorious failure! We learn a great deal from our mistakes. Keep focused on your own successes, and the successes of others, as well.

- The key in a nutshell: You dream, you imagine. You create a plan, and within it is a great challenge, with many apparent obstacles. As you encounter these difficulties, these problems, you look at each one and ask, *What is the opportunity here? What is the benefit in this difficulty? What is the gift?* If you keep imagining, and keep looking for the opportunities, benefits, and gifts that come to you, you will succeed, without a doubt.

- Add any notes or quotes from this lesson and from the rest of the lessons that follow in this Course to your folder. In the first three lessons, we covered all of the essential ingredients in your folder — your ideal scene, your goals, your plan, your vocation, and your purpose. From here on throughout the Course, add anything at all you feel moved to put in your folder. Work with it in your own creative way to make it a tool that works for you.

Within every adversity

is an equal or greater benefit.

Within every problem

is an opportunity.

Even in the knocks of life

we can find great gifts.

. . . .

LIVE AND WORK IN
PARTNERSHIP WITH ALL

I began working with these ideas the day I turned thirty. I wrote down my ideal scene — my dream life five years into the future — and I began affirming that each goal embedded in the life of my dreams was now manifesting, in an easy and relaxed manner, in a healthy and positive way, in its own perfect time, for the highest good of all.

It took me about ten years to fully achieve my ideal scene. I had a successful publishing company. I had recorded several albums of music and written several books. I had a beautiful home and a loving family.

During the next ten years, I wrote *Visionary Business* and then, after that book was published, I discovered the work of the renowned scholar and futurist Riane Eisler — and she gave me a whole new understanding, a new vocabulary and perspective, a way to simplify and clarify my life and my life's work. She gave me a great key to success.

I realized that key was something I had understood for years, for it had been fundamental to the success I had achieved, and fundamental throughout *Visionary Business* —

but I hadn't had the exact words for it, and so couldn't really see it or communicate it clearly until I read her work. Like most great keys, it is simple, even obvious to most people:

KEY 75

*The more you live and work
in partnership with all, the happier,
healthier, and more successful you will be.*

THE CHALICE AND THE BLADE

I first met Riane Eisler when we produced a condensed audio version of her great, celebrated book *The Chalice and the Blade.* In the book, she shows us that beliefs about society and the world were very different even just a few hundred years ago, and *completely* different a few thousand years ago — a tiny blip on the scale of human evolution. And, most important, she gives us a model for a livable future — based on going back to our roots, rather than inventing something new.

It is called the *partnership model.*

A great key to success is to discover where in our lives the *dominator model* — symbolized by the blade — is operating, and discover how to move more fully into partnership, symbolized by the open cup of the chalice.

Nearly all the world history we were taught in school has been the history of the *blade* — the history of domination — the conquest of warrior societies, beginning with the Greeks and Romans.

World history — at least this is what I was taught — started in Sumer, "the cradle of civilization," but quickly moved to Greece, "the birthplace of democracy," where it all really started. Then it moved to Rome, then the rest of Europe, and finally America! It was the history of the people who dominated the world, told from their point of view. Learning this history in school consisted of memorizing a great many dates for a great many wars.

India and China were mentioned somewhere as having ancient cultures, but all we ever learned about them was that India had a caste system and strange religions, and China invented gun powder, but they only used it for fireworks, and never invented guns. Africa was "the dark continent," shrouded in mystery. We knew little about it, except for Egypt, a great civilization four thousand years ago, now dead, and baffling.

Latin America was hardly even mentioned in the world history I was taught. Australia was mentioned only as the place that was settled by British convicts.

The world history we were taught was the story of the conquerors. An endless procession of wars and conflict, because violence only leads to more violence and domination leads to endless conflict. In the last century, we took the dominator model to the extreme, killing millions of people in world wars and finally having the nuclear power to annihilate life on earth!

But Eisler proves without a doubt that very different societies flourished before the select few we studied in our world history, and these societies have even coexisted with warrior societies, in some form, right into modern times — societies symbolized by the *chalice*, by partnership rather than domination.

We need to apply principles of partnership in every aspect of our lives, in all our relationships — with our families, our businesses, our communities, our governments, and our world, as well as with nature and spirit. The more we live and work in partnership, the more harmony, rather than conflict, we create in our lives and in our world.

This is the Great Work ahead of us:
the reinvention, the re-creation of society
so it is built on partnership rather than domination.

Partnership — from our families to the family of nations. This is a great key to success.

THE POWER OF PARTNERSHIP

Riane Eisler goes much further with it all in *The Power of Partnership*. This book was an eye-opener for me: It simplifies a lot of complex problems, and helps make solutions appear, solutions that are *doable*.

Eisler gives us what she calls a *lens*, a way to view our lives and the world, and it is a powerful tool. Through this lens we see everything in our lives and in our world on a continuum, with perfect pure partnership on one end and total domination on the other. We see that every relationship we have expresses either partnership — with its respect, harmony, and love — or attempts at domination, with its endless conflict, fear, and need to control.

In *The Power of Partnership*, we look at every relationship in our lives in a series of expanding circles, beginning with our relationship with *ourselves,* then moving out to our intimate relationships, including family and intimate friends, our community and work relationships, our relationship with our nation and with our world, and with nature and spirit. It's very powerful to examine every one of these relationships in our lives and see whether partnership or domination is primarily at work.

Once we start viewing ourselves and our world through this lens, we can clearly see how the partnership model, with its underlying respect for all, is definitely the simplest, most intelligent, and by far the most fun way to go — in every area of our lives. And we see that our ongoing challenge is to break free of the dominator model, with its underlying need to control others, and its endless resulting conflict.

The partnership model involves finding creative win-win solutions to problems. It is based on the Golden Rule, a great key to success in itself, one that most of us have heard many times, but very few of us practice in our lives:

Do unto others   KEY 77
as you would have them do unto you.

The partnership model is based on respect, on an awareness of the great value, even sacredness, of all life. The dominator model is based on fear, and leads one person or group to attempt to exert control over another. In a system of domination, the result is endless struggle, endless conflict for everyone involved. In partnership, the result is harmony, respect, love, and an explosion of creativity and joy.

Which would you rather have?

No one would choose the system of domination if they knew they had an alternative, but most of us haven't been given the lens to see the world in this way, and so don't have the tools to break free of the dominator model and move more fully into partnership in all areas of our lives.

But now literally hundreds of millions of people worldwide have read Riane Eisler and/or encountered other people of vision — from Christ, Buddha, Gandhi, Martin Luther King, Jr., and Mother Teresa to Albert Einstein, Eckhart Tolle, Shakti Gawain, Barbara Marx Hubbard, Deepak . Chopra, James Allen, and Napoleon Hill, to name just a few — and many people have seen remarkable changes in their lives and in their world as a result. A great movement has been born, and is gaining momentum: a movement toward partnership in every significant area of our lives.

KEY 78   *Domination is the problem,*
partnership is the solution.

In the things that are working smoothly in our lives, we have already discovered the power of partnership. In the things in our lives that still have struggle and conflict, we need to look at where there are still old patterns of domination.

PARTNERSHIP IN EVERY RELATIONSHIP

It is definitely worthwhile to look at every significant relationship in our lives, and ask ourselves which model is operating, partnership or domination:

OUR RELATIONSHIP WITH OURSELVES: Are you in partnership with yourself, do you nurture and support yourself, or is some inner critic or critical parent beating you up, undermining your uniqueness, your creativity, your joy of life? We need to be as gentle and accepting with ourselves as we ideally want to be with our children and intimate friends, and forge better partnerships with the creative child and spirit and genius we all have within.

OUR INTIMATE RELATIONSHIPS with our lovers, family, and intimate friends: Is there domination? Or do we truly have partnerships with family and friends? Is there respect? Does everyone have a voice? Is love acknowledged, in some way?

OUR WORK AND COMMUNITY RELATIONSHIPS: Do we have supportive partnerships with those we work with? Or are we still involved in a subtle or obvious system of domination?

Smart, successful employers have partnerships with every employee, every customer, every supplier, every stockholder or owner, everyone they interact with in their communities. Valuable employees have partnerships with their employers, their customers, other employees — everyone they interact with as well. Successful artists realize they have a network of partnerships that help them create and promote and sell their work.

Do we work in partnership with those in our community? Is everyone respected, does everyone has a voice? How do we find creative solutions that respect the people and the environment of the community? How can our businesses better support the communities they're located in?

More and more creative partnerships are being developed on a community level that address the communities' problems. Community partnerships can resolve those problems.

OUR NATIONAL RELATIONSHIPS: Do we have a successful partnership with all other Americans? Are we working together as citizens of one great country?

Do we have a smooth working partnership with our government? In some ways our government has been a visionary partner, in other ways our government continues to act as an aggressor and dominator. Where is the system of domination still firmly in place, and where is partnership operating? How can we move from the current system to one of greater partnership for everyone involved?

We have endless challenges ahead of us — and that means endless opportunities, benefits, and gifts.

OUR INTERNATIONAL RELATIONSHIPS: How successful are our partnerships with all the other governments and citizens of the world? Where is our country a dominator and where is it a partner in the world arena? What can we do to bring our nation's actions closer to partnership with other nations? What can we do personally to live in greater partnership with the peoples of the world?

There are many answers to these questions, and within these answers again are opportunities, benefits, and gifts for all.

OUR RELATIONSHIP WITH NATURE: Dominator or partnership? Are we consuming too many resources? Or even the right resources? Are we living within the means of the ecosystem? We have a partnership with our mother Earth that cannot be ignored, and we must find the ways to change all of our current dominator-based behavior.

Once we have a partnership with nature, she has so much to give us, including the secrets of a life well lived.

OUR RELATIONSHIP WITH SPIRIT: Are we in partnership with our spirit? Are we fully aware that we have a spiritual nature as well as a physical, emotional, and mental nature? Do we acknowledge and respect our spiritual nature? Do we let it guide us in our lives?

Do we respect the spiritual choices others have made?

KEY 79   *To fully realize the promise of this Course —*
living the life of our dreams —
we have to apply the partnership model
in every relationship we have.

FREEING OURSELVES FROM DOMINATION

Breaking free of the dominator model in all of our vast array of relationships offers us plenty of challenges and obstacles —

yet as we've seen, repeatedly, buried within these obstacles are great opportunities for a better life and a better world.

When we look for these opportunities, *all of us* can find practical solutions to our problems. When we look at our lives and the world in terms of partnership or domination, respect or control, we discover the tools to make a huge difference in the quality of our lives — and even in the evolution of our world. It doesn't matter whether we consider ourselves to be conservative or liberal, religious or secular, communist or capitalist, worker or employer, rich or poor, or categorized with any other current label for the divisions between us that you might care to name. So many of our problems stem from old traditions of domination — and the solution to all these problems is found in creative new ways of partnership.*

We can make it an affirmation — feel free to change the words in any way you wish:

> *All my relationships are loving partnerships —*   KEY 80
> *my life and my world are better and better,*
> *every day, in every way.*

PARTNERSHIP WITH EMPLOYEES

IF YOU'RE AN EMPLOYEE

Make sure you're in partnership with other employees, as well as your employer, customers, and everyone else you deal

---

* See *The Power of Partnership: Seven Relationships that Will Change Your Life* by Riane Eisler (New World Library, 2002), and also *The Chalice and the Blade: Our History, Our Future* (HarperSanFrancisco, 1988; an excellent condensation of the book on audiotape, edited and read by the author, is published by New World Library).

with. You're all on the same team: you all have the same goal of creating a successful business and fulfilling lives.

If you don't have a right-thinking employer who understands the power of the partnership model, respectfully but firmly lobby for the employee benefits below, which *every* business should have, whether large or small.

IF YOU'RE AN EMPLOYER

Practice partnership in every way you can. It's by far the best way to operate — the finest, easiest, healthiest, most fun way to build a business.

Keep this in mind: Your whole company reflects your consciousness. If you are, on a deep level, still fearful and feel a sense of scarcity and struggle, if you believe it's "everyone for themselves," and you have to hoard as much as possible for future security, you may think that your company isn't able to adequately provide for its employees, and you can't afford to give the kind of benefits an employee deserves — benefits you certainly want for yourself. If you feel this way, your company will reflect your fears, and you'll find yourself in constant struggle.

If this is the case, the most important work you have to do is within yourself. Do some honest self-examination. Ask yourself these questions, and look at the answers you come up with:

- Do I have an underlying belief that business has to be a struggle? Is it necessary to struggle in business? Is it helpful or useful?
- Do I have an underlying belief that our world is one of scarcity, and so I have to hoard as much as possible for future security for myself and my family?

- Do I have an underlying fear behind many of my thoughts and actions?
- Can I imagine creating a business that works smoothly, with an underlying harmony and enjoyment, rather than one filled with conflict, with an underlying struggle and fear and attempt to control?

If you want to be really successful as an employer,   KEY 81
set it up so your employees get rich.

In the process, you'll create a great success — a business filled with partnerships of inestimable value.

A POINT TO PONDER

There are many very successful people who are not struggling in the same way that most people are. They prove that other options are available — and we can choose an option that works better for all concerned. That option is called partnership.

I have tried for years to move toward greater partnership in my company, New World Library. My book *Visionary Business* can be summed up as my attempt to instill the partnership model into the business world. As a result, I have a company that runs so smoothly I don't even have to show up — it continues perfectly well on its own, with or without my input or support.

I have found over and over that when I believe in someone's abilities — when I see the full side of the glass, their greatest potential — they end up proving me right and demonstrating those abilities. Creative, competent people handle everything in my company, so I am free to do what I'm best at: focusing on the big picture, coming up with new

ideas, writing, speaking here and there, editing projects I
enjoy, playing music, goofing off — and having a family
life and personal life as well, with lots of time for solitude,
rest, and relaxation.

With the partnership model, things work so harmo-
niously and smoothly that it soon becomes obvious a much
greater force is at work, a powerful whole that is much greater
than the sum of its parts. Working in partnership inevitably
surrounds me with people who are far more capable than I
am at what they do. Working in partnership, with love and
respect for all, unleashes the creative force of the universe,
and it is bigger than all of us combined.

CONSCIOUSLY CHOOSING ABUNDANCE

Being aware of the prosperity and abundance available to
us helps us move into partnership more easily and gracefully.
Later on (in Lesson 8) we'll look in depth at the power of our
beliefs and see how, even when they are not true in themselves, they become self-fulfilling for us if we believe them. It's
very important, then, to ask ourselves this core question:

Do we live in an abundant world, or is it one of scarcity
and lack?

The irony is that some people live in a perfectly abundant world while others live in scarcity — and that we have
the power, whether we know it or not, to choose which
world to live in.

In fact, we *do* choose the world we live in, but for most
of us, the decision is subconscious — we're not even aware
we have made the decision to live in a world of scarcity and
lack. We're not even aware that we have decided in advance
what our level of income and our lifestyle will be. It was, up
until now, an almost entirely unconscious choice.

We can make it a *conscious* choice. As Barbara Marx Hubbard makes so clear in *Conscious Evolution,* it is our choice whether we want to improve our lives, whether we want to evolve, whether we will have a more fulfilling, peaceful, and satisfying life experience.

Up to now, most of us have chosen unconsciously, and many of our choices have been affected by poor, limited beliefs, all of them based on fear. We now realize we no longer need to make the same old choices, over and over. We realize we have the tools — you're holding one right now — to make new choices that result in a far more expansive, abundant, fulfilling way of life.

I can think of no finer lens to see the world through KEY 82
than conscious evolution.
It expands our horizon to see humanity
moving toward a higher dimension of life itself.

— **Barbara Marx Hubbard**
Conscious Evolution

IT'S SIMPLER THAN YOU THINK

I realized one day that attaining true, deep, lasting success — as I choose to define it — is really much simpler than I used to think it was. Having a mansion on a hill has nothing to do with it. Having a growing, balanced portfolio has nothing to do with it.

In fact, nothing out there in the world has anything to do with deep, lasting success and fulfillment. All the rewards are really found within us, within our minds and inner spirit, and so the most important work is within us as well. The work is in creating ever-better partnerships with ourselves and our spirit.

It might be much simpler than you think to create a successful, wonderfully fulfilling life for yourself. Most likely you don't need all the stuff you think you need in order to achieve the happiness, satisfaction, and fulfillment you are ultimately looking for.

What do you want ultimately?

Let's think it through: Many of us taking this Course, and many others throughout the world, want more income. Certainly financial security is a worthwhile goal.

But what do you want all that money for? We think that money will make us happy, content, but as soon as we make any money we discover that it brings no lasting happiness. Yes, there are sweet, heady moments when the big checks first roll in, when our first major goal is achieved, but those moments pass quickly, and we find we're the same people with the same number of problems, and the size of our bank account doesn't change that one bit. Having money doesn't affect all our habitual ways of thinking and usual ways of acting; it doesn't affect our ways of being.

When you use these tools and make the money you want, you'll discover this for yourself. For many people, this is depressing. But it doesn't have to be that way at all, for it can lead us to a great key to success and happiness if we look at it in the right way:

KEY 83

We don't need money to be happy or fulfilled.
In fact, money has nothing to do with it.

Once we understand this, isn't it good news? We can do what we want, and be who we want, and we may not have to change our financial picture at all. We might need more money to *have* what we think we want, but having these things, we soon discover, isn't important: It is *who we are* and *what we do* — it's our doing and being, not our having — that ultimately matters in life.

GRACE, EASE, AND LIGHTNESS

What do you want ultimately? Who are you in your ideal scene? I always get a picture of someone strolling peacefully around a quiet yard, feeling perfectly content. Someone fulfilled, living with *grace, ease, and lightness.*

What do you want, deep down? Contentment? Peace of mind? Fulfillment? Can you describe it in your own words?

Once we learn a few of these keys and apply a few of these tools, we can take a shortcut to success: We can have the fulfilling life we dream of *now,* in this moment. We see that the necessary work is inner work — and that makes it much easier than doing all that outer work we thought we had to do. As we have seen before, once we get the inside right, the outside takes care of itself.

A great key to this inner work is given in *The Power of Now* by Eckhart Tolle. It's worth repeating until we remember it, and live it — I've been reflecting on this phrase every day for over two years now:

> *To offer no resistance to life*   KEY 84
> *is to be in a state of grace, ease, and lightness.*
>
> — Eckhart Tolle, *The Power of Now*

Keep in mind that Eckhart is talking about our *inner* resistance to what is, rather than actions of resistance in the outer world. He doesn't mean we shouldn't be activists, or we shouldn't speak up and confront injustice and unfairness when we see it. But he shows us so clearly that the answers to our problems are found by letting go of the resistance we have within us and accepting what is — regardless of what we do in the outer world, even as we work for positive change.

When we offer no resistance to life, a great shift happens in our awareness, and in our whole physical, mental, and emotional being. Eckhart uses three beautiful words to describe what happens: *Grace, ease, and lightness.*

Aren't these the things you want in your ideal scene, ultimately, underneath everything else?

What good is being a millionaire if you're miserable? What good is having a great deal of stuff if you are constantly agitated, or endlessly driven to get more stuff, and fix that stuff, and maintain that stuff, and never find the time to relax and enjoy life?

No one on their deathbed has ever said, "I wish I would have made more money." No one on their deathbed has ever said, "I wish I would have spent more time at the office."

We are all going to be on our deathbeds far sooner than most of us wish. Are you going to have regrets? What can you do today to live your life in a way that will allow you to die peacefully? These questions are not morbid — they lead us to discover what is truly important in our lives. They lead to a life well lived.

James Allen was, as usual, tremendously insightful about this:

KEY 85

> *The more tranquil we become,*
> *the greater is our success, our influence,*
> *our power for good.*

> — James Allen, *As You Think*

EMPLOYEE BENEFITS

The owners and managers of truly successful companies —
companies that are a fulfilling experience for those involved
with them — live in a world of abundance. There is plenty
for all, and that includes all employees. Good employers remember the visionary advice Henry Ford gave: He said he
paid his auto workers much better than he could have paid
them because he needed them to be wealthy enough to afford
his cars. This is the vision that created the great American
middle class, and the tremendous prosperity our nation has
enjoyed.

Good employers remember the Golden Rule, and treat
their employees as they would wish to be treated if they
were employees. They understand this great bottom-line
fact: The partnership model is far more effective than
the old dominator model; the result is a more successful
company.

There is a very good reason for all of the following employee benefits: they all help the bottom line. The result of
having an excellent benefits package is that it retains excellent
people in your company, and the bottom line is enhanced as
a result. It is a win-win arrangement: Give your employees
great benefits, and they'll help you create far more profits
than those benefits cost. This has been proven over and over,
in my experience and in the experience of many other employers as well. Employees who are well rewarded stay with
the company and become valuable assets to that company,
and everyone wins as a result.

This is an important key to success, brilliantly stated by
H.S.M. Burns:

KEY 86

*Take care of those who work for you
and you'll soar to greatness on their achievements.*

— H.S.M. Burns

A fulfilling partnership with employees certainly includes everything in the list that follows.

RESPECT. Every person in the company deserves respect. There are no exceptions to this rule.

At New World Library, we state this (and the other benefits that follow) clearly in writing in the employee handbook everyone is given when they join the team. Everyone deserves to be listened to; no one deserves to be shouted at. It is a cause for termination in our company if one employee swears at another, or in other ways shows disrespect. Respect is the most basic quality of the partnership model; fear and the need to control, with its resultant inevitable disrespect, are the basic qualities of the dominator model.

A CHANCE TO GROW ON THE JOB. Treat people like adults, give them opportunities to grow, and their productivity will soar. Make them managers of their position — regardless of the job — and give them the challenge of improving their contribution to the company.

Invite them to add their creative ideas to the mix. Create an environment that encourages brainstorming on all kinds of ideas — thinking outside of the box — and even encourages disagreement without fear of some kind of disapproval. This is the partnership model in action.

LIVABLE WAGES. The book *Fast Food Nation* points out that a great number of big businesses have a policy of hiring mainly part-time people at low wages and giving them no benefits. This is just plain stupid; it is a shortsighted business policy. It leads to a badly run business. These employers don't understand what Henry Ford understood; they don't understand the power of partnership.

Every business should pay its employees a livable wage and give them a full benefits package as well: Isn't it obvious to everyone how much better a business thrives when employees are treated well? The increased efficiency, energy, and enthusiasm that come from well-trained, motivated employees contribute substantially to a company's financial success, and more than pay for employee benefits. To have a win-win partnership with your employees, you've obviously got to pay them a wage they can live on.

GENEROUS PAID VACATIONS. Isn't that what you want? Isn't that what everybody wants? Every company should make it a priority. In the long run, it's even cost effective, for vacations are great therapy that help prevent chronic stress, illness, and burnout. And, as everyone knows, the best ideas for solving problems and the most expansive ideas for growing the business are often discovered on vacations.

If you're a business owner, don't forget to take vacations yourself! It may be the best thing you can do for your business, in the long run.

MEDICAL AND DENTAL INSURANCE. This is essential for everyone. Either employers or the government should provide it. In Scandinavia, there is medical and dental coverage for all, and even free day care for children, courtesy of governments that are far closer to an enlightened partnership model than ours is. In Denmark they pay much higher prices for gasoline than we do, but most people are all for it because the taxes on gas pay for free health care for all. Until our government wakes up and gets it right, employers have to make medical and dental insurance a priority.

PENSION PLANS. Put into place the best pension plan you can find. This benefit builds longevity and loyalty, and retains top-quality employees.

We chose the finest plan available: a profit-sharing pension plan. Each year we fully vest the plan, and from 10 to 15 percent of an employee's annual income is paid by the company from its profits and put into the employee's pension fund. It costs the employee nothing, and builds tax-free over time. With it, employees are automatically saving 10 to 15 percent of their base salary, building in tax-sheltered, diversified investments for their future. They can borrow against it for housing, education for themselves or their children, or medical expenses not covered by insurance.

This kind of plan does wonders for employee morale. It's another one of the reasons why we have almost no employee turnover at our company — people very rarely leave. Some employees have told me they want to keep their jobs for the rest of their working lives!

PROFIT SHARING. *All* businesses should have profit sharing, even the tiniest operations with just one employee. Profit sharing should include everyone working for the company, including part-time workers. McDonald's should have profit sharing; the post office should have profit sharing.

There's no excuse for not doing it — it's just good business. Every employee, once given a share of the profits, begins to act like an owner, and every employee has the ability to help the company's bottom line: to cut costs and/or increase income. In the long run, far more profits are made by the company — so owners make more money if they share profits generously. Everyone wins in the deal.

Profit sharing instills pride of ownership in employees. It vastly improves their performance, and the bottom line improves as well. Profit sharing turns a mediocre employee into a good employee, a good employee into an excellent one, and an excellent employee into a creative, visionary force that helps the company immensely.

These words are not just theory: they have been proven true by experience. Here's another way to summarize it: The partnership model is more powerful than the dominator model.

BOTTOM LINE

Treat employees like adults, with respect, and they'll shine in their performance. Consider them managers, and treat them all like managers, for every employee manages *something*. Invite them to add ideas to the company's ongoing plans for the future.

Give them clear, challenging goals, and then let them do their job in their own creative way. Learn to delegate rather than to micro-manage. That way, you empower your people to remarkable heights of creativity and performance.

Treat employees like valuable assets to the company   KEY 87
and they will become valuable assets.

A PROFIT-SHARING FORMULA

Tailor a specific profit-sharing formula that works for your company. We model ours on a Swiss hotel I happened to read about in an in-flight airline magazine. They were losing money, and wanted to hire a new manager. The best candidate for the job said that if he were hired, he would insist on retaining a third of the profits for expansion and growth, and split the rest equally between employees and owners. At first the owners objected, but the manager reminded them they weren't making any money; in fact, they were losing it rapidly! So they went along with the profit-sharing program.

When the employees heard they would share in the profits, there was an immediately noticeable shift in their energy and attitudes. At the end of the first year, they received a cash bonus equal to two weeks' pay. Seven years later, when the article was written about them, employees received a bonus equal to seven-and-a-half months' pay.

The new manager had created a win-win arrangement that made everyone happy — employees, owners, and customers.

That arrangement seems perfectly balanced to me, fair to all, and easy to implement: We retain about a third in the company for growth — this number varies depending on what our banker and accountant suggest — and then we split the rest of the profits 50–50 between employees and owners.

It's a true win-win scenario: We give a generous piece of the pie to the employees and the whole pie expands as a result, so owners end up making more than they would if they had kept the whole pie to themselves.

Besides, it's a lot more fun working with motivated, creative people than with employees who are just watching the clock and worrying about how to pay for a new set of tires or their child's dental bill.

KEY 88

As an employer, you have the power to ensure that every long-term employee amasses wealth and builds an abundant future.

A SIMPLE EXAMPLE

A small, struggling company had an office near ours. I got to know some of the staff there, and they would often launch into their complaints about the company in general and their boss in particular. They didn't have any sort of profit sharing and had very few other benefits, and the employees were dissatisfied, turnover was high, and productivity was low.

One of the employees asked me to give the owner a copy of *Visionary Business,* and the owner read it and then asked me how to implement profit sharing. I said anything would do for a start — she could start simply by passing out $100 to each employee and announcing they were going to begin sharing some percentage of the profits. She wouldn't even have to come up with the exact percentage yet, just promise *something.*

A few months later she told me she was *amazed* at the changes in the company since that one little bit of profit sharing: Sales had increased dramatically, and profits had more than doubled, because employees were not only passively filling orders, but encouraging customers to order other related things. Best of all, the entire corporate culture had changed. People were taking on more responsibility and finding new creative ways to improve the bottom line. It was a lot more fun to work there.

Everybody wins, in so many ways, when management moves toward partnership with employees. With these benefits, you release a flood of joyous creativity that improves the business in every way and makes life in general a lot more fun.

A key that encompasses many of these things could be expressed in this way:

> *Work in partnership with others*
> *to help them realize their dreams.*
> *Then you will have all kinds of support*
> *for realizing your dreams as well.*

KEY 89

RECEIVING THE BENEFITS OF PARTNERSHIP

To receive the full effects of the benefits of partnership, use the term "employees" to mean anyone and everyone you're working with, including the plumber at your house, the person who does your tax returns, your child's teacher, your waiter or waitress, even the people who cold-call you and try to sell you something over the phone — in short, anyone and everyone you interact with throughout the day.

In other words,

KEY 90

*Work in partnership with yourself
and with everyone else you encounter
throughout the day.*

We all have great challenges in our lives, and there is great work to do: we need to reinvent and re-create our society so it is built on partnership rather than domination.

A FEW BOTTOM-LINE QUESTIONS

Let's review again from a different angle: Ask yourself these questions, and give yourself some time to see what answers arise:

*   What do I want for myself, ultimately in my life?
*   What do I hope to have achieved, to have become, as I look back on my life just before that great transition we call death?
*   Do I have a final, single goal in life? If so, does it affect the way I am today? Am I affirming that goal regularly?

KEY 91

*The Force that guides the stars
guides you too.*

— P. R. Sarkar

Add any notes or quotes from this lesson that you particularly want to remember to your folder.

SUMMARY

- One of the most powerful and rewarding things we can do is to look at every relationship in our lives — including our relationships with *ourselves,* our families and intimate friends, our work and community, our nation, our world, nature, and spirit — and see whether we're primarily working in partnership or whether there is some form of domination in effect.

- The more you live and work in partnership with all, the happier, healthier, and more successful you will be. Living and working in partnership is far more fun than being trapped in exploitation and domination, with its endless conflict and resentment.

- A great key to success is to discover where there is domination and exploitation in our lives, and discover how to move more fully into partnership with all.

- Domination creates the problems; partnership provides the solutions.

- This is the Great Work ahead of us: the reinvention, the re-creation of society so it is built on partnership rather than domination.

Work in partnership with others

to help them realize their dreams.

Then you will have all kinds of support

for realizing your dreams as well.

LESSON 6

. . . .

AVOID MANAGEMENT BY CRISIS
WITH CLEAR GOALS
AND TRANSPARENCY

WAYS TO AVOID MANAGEMENT BY CRISIS

There are two popular styles of management: management by crisis and management by goals.

Those who are caught in crisis management have become so focused on the day-to-day problems they rarely have time to step back and see the big picture. They're working *in* the business and never have time to work *on* the business. Day-to-day details and worries have become all-consuming, and their vision of the future is lost. Their anxieties have eroded their dream — and, if not checked, can destroy that dream entirely.

A dream is a fragile thing —
yet it can be the most powerful thing in the world.

KEY 92

Dreams are like tiny infants in many ways: They have the power to quickly grow, but they are small and vulnerable, and need to be constantly watched and protected. If they aren't, they won't survive.

Our dreams need to be continually reinforced so they

become firmly rooted in our subconscious. Doubts and fears and challenges and obstacles will arise, and they need to be acknowledged, observed, and dealt with (see Lesson 8 for more on this). When we do this, what happens is magical: Our dreams begin to grow into reality.

As our dreams come into being, we inevitably have to manage them in some way. If we're focusing primarily on the half-empty part of the glass, we have management by crisis. When we focus on the half-full side, we can manage with clear goals and confident optimism.

There are twelve fundamental ways to avoid management by crisis — many of them are covered more extensively in other lessons.

1
TAKE BREAKS FROM THE DAY-TO-DAY DETAILS

Get away occasionally. Take a break. Do nothing for at least a little while. Relax. Take some "R and R," as they say in the military — relaxation and recreation. Discover the rejuvenating power of relaxation.

Go on a retreat for a day, a week, a month. Take a mini-retreat of half a day, or even an hour. Mondays are especially good for retreats — so good that I take almost every Monday as a retreat, a day to do nothing at all, to do whatever I feel like in the moment. I take mini retreats almost every morning as well.

Think of your home as your spa, and take a long, hot bath.

So many of us have forgotten the great value and pleasure of having a day of rest. Even God needed a day of rest. The tradition of the Sabbath is a great one: having one day

. . . .

a week set aside as holy, a day to do no work, a day of rest and prayer.

As our indigenous friends remind us, every day of the week is holy. Yet there is still a great value in regularly setting one day aside for relaxation. It is rejuvenating, in its fullest sense — healing, even inspiring.

2
MAKE A PLAN

Plan your business. Have a clear plan in mind, preferably in writing, for the next year. Then have a more expansive plan: What do you want to be doing five years from now?

Take some time to work *on* the business, rather than *in* the business. Schedule the first steps toward your plan on your daily or monthly calendar, and begin taking those steps.

Then take another break, and relax for a while. Take it easy, partner.

3
MAKE CLEAR GOALS, AND AFFIRM
THOSE GOALS REGULARLY

I read about a Korean billionaire who gets up early every morning and spends an hour writing his goals, over and over. If you have the discipline to do that (I don't), I know it would very quickly have a great effect on your life. It's a good example of a completely nonspiritual way to use these tools: There is no prayer, no belief in a higher power, you simply put your goals in writing, over and over.

An hour a day isn't necessary — even an hour a month

can have a great effect. Make a list of goals and affirm your goals, repeatedly, adding these powerful words:

KEY 23

In an easy and relaxed manner,
In a healthy and positive way,
In its own perfect time,
For the highest good of all.

Do whatever is necessary for you to keep your goals in mind. That's all you need to do. The universe takes care of the rest.

Just by making and repeating your goals, all kinds of possibilities, opportunities, and plans naturally emerge, all by themselves — and the next step to take to move closer to your goals becomes obvious and easy.

4
WORK IN PARTNERSHIP WITH ALL

We have seen in our lives that when we work in partnership, we discover ways to turn conflict into harmony. Treat others as you wish to be treated, and management by crisis will naturally evolve into management by teamwork and partnership.

Everyone is a winner when there is partnership all around. The Dodo Bird in *Alice in Wonderland* said it very well:

KEY 93

Everyone has won,
and all must have prizes!

— Lewis Carroll, *Alice in Wonderland*

That's a great management principle. Everyone in the organization has already won, just by virtue of working there, and all must have prizes, preferably in substantial amounts of cash, but also in generous benefits and paid vacations — and now more and more companies are even giving paid leave to people for volunteer work. (This is a great development — it is helping change the world.)

Exploitation and domination create endless problems; the only lasting solutions are found by working in partnership.

5
LOOK AT THE HALF-FULL SIDE
OF THE GLASS

We have looked at this key extensively as well. Acknowledge the crisis, the problems, the difficulties, the obstacles, but then ask yourself: What are the opportunities here? What are the benefits? What are the gifts? What are the possibilities?

Brainstorm freely. Write a list of *What Ifs*. Think of possible ways the crisis could be resolved, in a healthy and positive way, for the highest good of all.

Just by making a list of possible solutions, you are well on your way to creating the solutions you need.

6
KEEP PICTURING SUCCESS

Those who fail have a clearer picture of failure than of success. As Steven Covey put it in *Seven Habits of Highly Effective People,* "Begin with the end in mind." And keep that end in mind, through all the cycles of change that we inevitably experience as we build something over time.

We create the life of our dreams as soon as our picture of

it becomes more dominant in our thoughts and subconscious than our picture of how difficult it is to achieve it.

At some point in the process, our dreams become clear goals — and then our goals become intentions. Once we have a solid, unwavering intention, success is inevitable. Along the way we may fail over and over again, but each failure simply brings us closer to success.

7

LEARN THE GREAT VALUE OF TRANSPARENCY

It was Neale Donald Walsch, author of *Conversations with God,* who first used the word "transparency" in a way that was new for me: In all your business dealings, he said, you should be so completely honest that you are transparent, so the others involved know exactly what kind of energy and resources you're putting into any given project, and what kind of return you expect, and you know exactly what energy and resources they're putting in, and what they expect to get in return.

Successful business is not a poker game, where you're hiding your hand — and it is certainly not a game of Monopoly, where you're trying to drive someone else into bankruptcy. A business (or an artist) that is truly successful in the long run creates a series of flourishing partnerships, and everyone involved supports each other, is willing to give and compromise, and has an open hand.

I show you my cards, and you show me yours; together we work it out so we both win the game. It's much more fun when everyone is a winner, and no one is a loser.

This is a great key to success.

8
DON'T THINK TOO SMALL

Don't let doubts, fears, and "small thinking" undermine your goal. If you think small, whatever you create will remain small.

Your business — in whatever form it takes — reflects your mind. Your business is the sum of all the thoughts you've had about it. It reflects your dominant visualization. Think expansively. Start with your *ideal* scene — what do you want ideally?

The great key Deepak Chopra gave us in *Creating Affluence* is worth repeating:

Within every desire   KEY 58
is the seed and mechanics for its fulfillment.
— **Deepak Chopra**, *Creating Affluence*

This is a key to success, worth remembering.

9
LEARN HOW TO SETTLE ARGUMENTS

In crisis, arguments flare. At the core of every argument is always the fact that someone feels they're not being heard by the other. Arguments are fueled by constant interruptions. Everyone is trying so hard to make their point that they're not listening to anyone else. When we work together in partnership, arguments can always be resolved, because everyone is given attention and respect. If you're working with someone as their partner, you always listen to what they say and take it into consideration. Everyone has their say.

The key to resolving arguments is learning to listen *without interrupting*.

Over the years we developed a simple technique for settling arguments. It works. Within it is a great key to effective, satisfying personal and business relationships:

KEY 94

There's no need for argument —
in fact it's not an effective form of communication at all.
There is a much better alternative: listening,
and working in partnership.

THE ARGUMENT-SETTLING TECHNIQUE

If you find yourself in an argument, go through these steps:

1. STOP ARGUING AND LISTEN TO THE OTHER PERSON.

Once you start arguing, you're getting nowhere. Nothing has ever been resolved in the heat of an argument. Both of you are trying so hard to be heard that neither one is open to hearing what the other is trying to say. So just stop, and let the other person have their say; let them completely express themselves without interrupting them, and without denying what they're saying, defending yourself, or putting yourself or the other person down in any way.

Just listen to what they're saying, take it in, and accept it as being exactly what they need to say at that moment. This is difficult to do at first, but it's a great skill to master, for it effectively resolves arguments and also empowers you in the process.

When you stop arguing and just listen quietly to the other person, what they have to say — even in the most heated arguments — very rarely takes more than two or three minutes. Give them a few minutes of your time, *without interrupting.*

2. NOW IT'S YOUR TURN TO EXPRESS YOUR THOUGHTS AND FEELINGS, AS COMPLETELY AS POSSIBLE.

You've listened to them, now ask them to listen to you, without interrupting. You'll give them another chance to speak their peace, but now you want to speak yours. Again it rarely takes more than two or three minutes.

3. LISTEN TO THEIR RESPONSE, WITHOUT INTERRUPTING.

You'll have more chances to respond; for now, just listen. This steps rarely takes more than a minute or two.

4. RESPOND.

These last two steps may be repeated as many times as necessary — let the other person speak, then you speak, without being interrupted. It's rarely necessary to repeat these steps more than two or three times. You'll know when you're ready to move on to the next step.

5. ASK WHAT THE OTHER PERSON WANTS FROM YOU.

Listen without interrupting. Every argument is based on the fact that the people involved aren't getting what they want.

6. TELL THE OTHER PERSON EXACTLY WHAT YOU WANT FROM HIM OR HER.

Be as honest and direct as possible. Make it as clear as possible. Now you're ready for the final step.

7. NEGOTIATE AND MAKE CLEAR AGREEMENTS.

Compromise may be necessary for one or both of you, but keep negotiating until you reach an agreement you're both satisfied with — a win-win agreement. You might have to do some creative brainstorming here, go through a few *What Ifs,* but there is some creative solution that works for both of you. You will find it if you keep talking without interrupting each other.

The argument-settling technique is simple to explain, but not easy to do. When I first did this process, I had to struggle not to interrupt, and I even used a notebook and made quick notes of what was said, so I could remember to respond to every point. After going through the process a few times, I realized there was no need at all to respond to everything, and notes were completely unnecessary. Just respond to whatever comes to mind when it's your turn to talk.

It's all right to take notes, if you want, as long as you keep listening and don't interrupt — and don't deny what the other person is saying, or defend yourself, or put yourself or the other person down in any way, not even through unspoken body language.

THE SIMPLIFIED ARGUMENT-SETTLING TECHNIQUE

There is a simple way to use this technique:

If you're involved in the argument, just stop interrupting, and listen to the other person. When they're through, ask them not to interrupt you, just as you didn't interrupt them, and speak your peace.

If two other people are involved in the argument, you can step in and referee, insisting on just one rule: They talk to each other without interrupting each other. You may have to remind them at some point not to interrupt. It works every time: You simply cannot have an argument if you sit and listen to each other.

When you discover how to listen to someone, to anyone, without responding immediately, especially without rushing to deny or defend, you become a changed person.

If you do this exercise, I promise you'll discover something amazingly powerful — and those words aren't too strong to describe the effects of this simple process.

10
AVOID LAWSUITS

Most lawsuits add to the load of problems rather than creating effective solutions. They are a foolish waste of time and money, and they are unnecessary when we work in partnership and learn how to settle arguments. Our system of litigation is to be avoided at all costs, because it's a dominator-based system. It is a fight; it is war. War needs to be resolved through mediation, which involves finding creative compromises that work for all parties involved.

If you ever have a conflict you can't resolve on your own, find a good mediator and work it out. Mediation is partnership based.

Our contracts have a clause that says any and all conflicts will be resolved between the parties in a spirit of respect and cooperation, with a willingness to compromise; if we can't work it out, we will go to a mediator. If that fails, we agree to go to legally binding arbitration, and resolve it there.

In over twenty-five years of business, I've never had to go to arbitration. I've gone to small claims court one time, when our business was in its infancy, as a very last resort in collecting from someone who owed us. It involved no lawyers and was a good experience: a simple process that took little time or expense. I've never been involved in any other litigation.

I have used a mediator on one occasion, and it was a very positive experience for all concerned, a wonderful example of the partnership model: We found a way to get what both of us wanted and yet fully support the other person in getting what they wanted. We came up with a creative solution that was definitely a win-win for all involved.

The partnership model leads to harmony rather than conflict, and the process of mediation resulted in harmony and good feelings — and we continue to this day to work together creatively and enjoyably.

11
UNDERSTAND AND MASTER TIME

Most of us have heard the old adage that our work expands to fill the time we allot to it. Most of us have seen it happen in our professional lives. We make an assumption about how much time we need to devote to our career, and before we know it our assumption has come true. We rarely stop to ask if perhaps, like many of our core beliefs, that assumption has become a self-fulfilling prophesy. If you believe you need to work sixty to eighty hours a week to survive, you'll end up doing it.

To me, that's inhumane. I give my company between thirty and forty hours a week of focused attention, and that's enough. My work shrinks to fill the time I give to it. When we understand this principle, we can master time.

We can express this key by paraphrasing James Allen's great poem in *As You Think:*

KEY 95

> *The human will — that force unseen,*
> *the offspring of a deathless soul —*

is able to master time, and even conquer space, chance,
environment, and circumstances.

Understanding time, and even mastering time, is not an impossible task. It involves looking at our beliefs about time and being willing to change some of those old beliefs. There are many people who have a very different experience of time in their lives, including most of the indigenous people on this earth.

Why do people in so many other cultures have so much time to hang out and enjoy life? If they can do it, why can't you? I have a lot of free time by myself to do whatever I want in the moment — usually more time than I spend at work, in fact — and if I can do it, why can't you?

There's an eye-opening book called *Simply Living: The Spirit of the Indigenous Peoples,* edited by Shirley Ann Jones. In it, a woman says she finds it very strange that her daughter, who has moved to the city, has washing machines and all these other labor-saving devices, yet doesn't have time to come see her mother and just sit for the afternoon and talk.

How come the people with the labor-saving devices are running around doing so much work while so many of the people without them have all the time to spend as families and communities?

The answer to this question is found not in the devices we have, not anywhere, in fact, in the outside world, but rather in our beliefs about time. Different people have different sets of beliefs about time, and so live in a completely different reality.

It's odd when you think about it: We all have a large, complex set of beliefs about time, yet we almost never think about those beliefs, and rarely — if ever — examine them consciously. When we do give them some thought, we soon realize that, like all our other beliefs, they are not necessarily true in themselves — but they are self-fulfilling *if we believe them to be true.*

By looking at our beliefs (there's more on specifically how to do this in Lesson 8) we discover we can affect those beliefs, we can change those beliefs — and our reality changes as a result.

Until I was thirty-five or so, I believed that there wasn't enough time — or money — in my life. The two were related somehow, and I struggled with both of them. For some reason, God didn't create enough. Time was always passing me by. There wasn't enough to time to do what I wanted to do. I kept noticing that things would always take so much more time than I planned on. Time was flying.

Do any of these beliefs sound familiar?

Then something shifted in my belief system. I found I could make a conscious choice to change my beliefs to create more time in my life. I'm almost certain that the single most effective thing I did was to keep affirming these words with my goals: *in an easy and relaxed manner, in a healthy and positive way, in its own perfect time.*

Now I have all the time I need in life. I rarely have to rush anywhere. I have plenty of free time, all the time for relaxation and rejuvenation that I want and need, all the time I want for my creative work, and plenty of time for friends and family. My entire experience of reality has shifted as my belief that I have enough has become dominant over my earlier belief of scarcity.

Are you often stressed, running some kind of race with the clock? What are you thinking, what are you telling yourself at the time?

Do you believe there is a shortage of time? Did the universe somehow not create enough for you?

Take a good look at your beliefs about time, and take the necessary steps to change them.

KEY 96

Affirm your goals are being realized
in an easy and relaxed manner,
in a healthy and positive way, in their own perfect time.
These words are true magic:
They can help you master time and money.

We are slaves to the clock only as long as we believe we are. We are perfectly capable of mastering time. Within these pages are the keys that show us how. We live in an abundant universe, and that includes an abundance of time, money, and everything else.

12
UNDERSTAND AND MASTER MONEY

Until I turned thirty-five, there certainly wasn't enough money in my life. I had a mass of confused beliefs about money. Money was hard to come by; money was scarce. Money doesn't grow on trees. I believed it took hard work, intelligence, talent, and perseverance to make money — things I didn't believe I had or wanted to do. I believed it took money to make money — and since I didn't have any money, the cards were stacked against me. The rich get richer and the poor get poorer. A fool and his money are soon parted — and I believed, deep down, when I looked at my history with money, I was a fool. It was certainly true in my experience: however much I made I quickly spent. Besides, I even felt that maybe money really is the root of all evil. Money corrupts. It is impossible for a rich person to be a good person.

Do any of these beliefs sound familiar to you?

It's odd when we think about it: We all have a large, complex set of beliefs about money, yet — just as with our beliefs about time — we almost never think about those beliefs. We almost never examine them consciously, and very rarely ask ourselves whether those beliefs are valid or really true.

Our beliefs about money are self-fulfilling, like all our other beliefs. They are not necessarily true in themselves — our thinking makes them so. Many people think differently, and have very different beliefs about money — doesn't that prove that our beliefs are not true in themselves, and can change over time? That has certainly been true in my experience.

What are you thinking, what are you telling yourself about money?

Do you believe there is a shortage of money? Did the universe somehow not create enough for you? Do you believe you don't have what it takes to make a substantial amount of money? Do you believe money is hard to get? Do you believe that if you get it, someone else will have to do without it, or in some other way be hurt by it? Do you believe money will corrupt you? Or distract you from the important things in life?

Take a good look at your beliefs about money, and take the necessary steps to change them. This Course is full of keys that show us how to do this. After I worked with this material for a while, something shifted in my belief system about money and its availability. I came to see and believe that money could be a tremendous force for good in my life, and in the lives of many others.

KEY 97

I found I could make a conscious decision
to change my beliefs
and create more money and more time in my life.
The choice was up to me.

I'm almost certain that the single most effective thing I did in this arena was to ask, to pray — whatever you want to call it — for a specific amount of money, one that was an expansive leap for me to even imagine.

As soon as I ask for an expansive amount of money, I begin to get creative new ideas, and different possibilities come to mind that could very well result in the kind of money I asked for. Different opportunities suddenly appear — and it often feels as though those opportunities had been right in front of me all along, but I just hadn't seen them before.

Some of these possibilities lead me to paths I don't want to take or have no interest in or energy for; some lead to prospects I reject because they don't feel easy, relaxed, healthy, or positive in some way; but some of the possibilities excite something in me, and take me in new directions that are challenging and fulfilling.

I have reached the point where I can honestly say I have all the money I need in life. The universe amply provides for me, for I realize that I live in a world that is truly abundant. I have discovered ways to create income streams from a wide variety of sources. I have enough passive income from investments in stock, bonds, and real estate to support me. I have received what I have asked for, no more, no less.

This is certainly a key:

> ### *You will receive what you ask for,* KEY 98
> ### *no more, no less.*

My entire experience of reality has shifted as newer beliefs gradually replaced my earlier beliefs of scarcity. I don't work for money any more; I do what I love and there is always plenty of money. This is what I believe, and this is what has come true in my life.

I'm not writing this book for the money. I'm writing it because I love this project, and have the desire and energy to do it. I'm doing it because I love the whole process of writing and publishing books. If it makes money, that's great; if it doesn't make a dime, that's okay too. The universe provides.

MONEY MAGIC

If, after you have been through this Course, you still have problems with money, I'd recommend you read and work with *Money Magic* by Deborah L. Price. She is an experienced and perceptive financial advisor, and shows us the eight possible "money types" — you can probably identify yourself just by her labels.

The goal is to move from your current money type to become a money magician.

- THE INNOCENT — We all start here; many stay stuck here.
- THE VICTIM — "It's not my fault." Forces beyond my control are always messing me up financially.
- THE WARRIOR — fights and conquers the money world. Often successful, rarely contented or satisfied with that success.
- THE MARTYR — denies oneself for others' needs.
- THE FOOL — gamblers and adventurers who are usually soon parted with the money that comes their way. (This was me, for years.)
- THE CREATOR/ARTIST — artistic or spiritual, ambivalent toward money, both attracted to it and repulsed by it. (This was my money type as well, from childhood until mid-thirties.)

- THE TYRANT — uses money to dominate and control. Has a life full of endless conflict as a result.
- THE MAGICIAN — the ideal — understands how to create money, how to ask for it and receive it. As it is said in *Money Magic:*

Using a new and ever-changing set of dynamics both in the material world and in the world of the Spirit, Magicians know how to transform and manifest their own financial reality.

At our best, when we are willing to claim our own power, we are all Magicians. Magicians are armed with the knowledge of the past, have made peace with their personal history, and understand that their source of power exists within their ability to see and live the truth of who they are.

Magicians know the source of power to manifest lies in their ability to tap into their Higher Power. With faith, love, and patience, Magicians simply wait in certainty with the knowledge that all our needs are met all the time.

Magicians embrace the inner life as the place of spiritual wealth and the outer life as the expression of enlightenment in the material world. They are infinitely connected.

> *Simply wait in certainty with the knowledge that all your needs are met all the time.*
>
> — **Deborah L. Price**, *Money Magic*

KEY 99

If that's too metaphysical for you and you still have money problems, read *Think and Grow Rich* by Napoleon Hill. It is filled with powerful tools to master money.

There is one place where Hill and I part ways, however: He says your desire for wealth must become a "single, burning obsession." That sounds to me a bit, well, *obsessive.* It sounds like something that would get in the way of a balanced and fulfilled life that includes time for friends, family, personal expression, and relaxation as well as making money.

I have realized, I have seen in my own life, that the following simple statement is true:

KEY 100

> *You can create money and whatever else you want*
> *in a sane, balanced way,*
> *in an easy and relaxed manner.*

There is no need whatsoever to have burning obsessions — clear goals, yes, affirmed in an easy and relaxed manner, in a healthy and positive way, but not all-consuming obsessions. We can have a balanced life, time for rest and relaxation as well as work.

Clearly state to the universe exactly what you desire. Then let it all go, and let the universe work out the details. Go about your day in an easy and relaxed manner, taking whatever steps are in front of you, in their own perfect time, for the highest good of all.

SUMMARY

- THERE ARE TWO POPULAR STYLES OF MANAGEMENT: management by crisis and management by goals. There are several fundamental ways to avoid management by crisis:
- TAKE BREAKS FROM THE DAY-TO-DAY DETAILS occasionally and relax and rejuvenate.

- MAKE A PLAN. Schedule the first steps toward your plan on your daily or monthly calendar, and begin taking those steps.
- MAKE CLEAR GOALS, AND AFFIRM THOSE GOALS REGULARLY. When affirming your goals, add these powerful words: *In an easy and relaxed manner, in a healthy and positive way, in its own perfect time, for the highest good of all.*
- WORK IN PARTNERSHIP WITH ALL, and you'll discover how to turn conflict into harmony. Treat others as you wish to be treated, and management by crisis will evolve over time into management by teamwork.
- LOOK AT THE HALF-FULL SIDE OF THE GLASS. Acknowledge the crisis, the problems, but then ask yourself, What are the opportunities here? What are the possibilities? Brainstorm freely. Make a list of possible ways the crisis could be resolved, in a healthy and positive way, for the highest good of all.
- KEEP PICTURING SUCCESS. Those who fail have a clearer picture of failure than of success. As Steven Covey put it, "Begin with the end in mind." And keep that end in mind, through all the cycles of change that we inevitably experience as we build something over time.
- LEARN THE GREAT VALUE OF TRANSPARENCY. In all your business dealings, be completely honest to the point of being transparent, so that the others involved know exactly what kind of energy and resources you're putting into the project, and what kind of return you expect, and you know exactly what energy and resources they're putting in, and what they expect to get in return.
- A business or artist that is truly successful in the long

run creates an ongoing series of win-win partnerships, and everyone involved supports each other, is
willing to give and compromise, and has an open
hand.

- DON'T THINK TOO SMALL. Don't let doubts, fears,
  and "small thinking" undermine your goals. If you
  think small, whatever you create will remain small.
  Think expansively. Start with your ideal scene —
  what do you want ideally?

- LEARN HOW TO SETTLE ARGUMENTS. There is a
  simple technique for this. It involves the very difficult
  but highly rewarding task of learning to listen to what
  someone else is saying, even when they're angry with
  you, *without interrupting* — and without denying
  what they're saying, defending yourself, or putting
  yourself or the other person down in any way.

- AVOID LAWSUITS. They are unnecessary. Our
  system of litigation is to be avoided, because it's a
  dominator-based system. It is a war. The only lasting
  solutions to war or any other conflicts are found
  through creative mediation with everyone involved.
  If you ever have a conflict you can't work out between yourselves, find a good mediator and work it
  out. Mediation is partnership-based. If that fails, go
  to binding arbitration rather than litigation.

- UNDERSTAND AND MASTER TIME. This is not an
  impossible task for people today. It involves looking at
  our beliefs about time and being willing to change
  some of those beliefs. There are many people who have
  a very different experience of time in their lives, including most of the indigenous peoples on this earth.

- I found I could make a conscious choice to change
  my beliefs to create more time in my life. I'm almost

certain that the single most effective thing I did was to keep affirming these words with my goals: *in an easy and relaxed manner, in a healthy and positive way, in its own perfect time.*

- UNDERSTAND AND MASTER MONEY. Our beliefs about money are self-fulfilling, like all our other beliefs. They are not necessarily true in themselves — our thinking makes them so. Many people have very different beliefs than you do about money — doesn't that prove that our beliefs are not true in themselves, and can change over time?

- Take a good look at your beliefs about money, and take the necessary steps to change them. This Course is full of keys that show us how to do this. After I worked with this material for a while something shifted in my belief system about money and its availability. *I found I could make a conscious decision to change my beliefs and create more money in my life. The choice was up to me.*

- I'm almost certain that the single most effective thing I did in this arena was to ask, to pray — whatever you want to call it — for a specific amount of money, one that was an expansive leap for me to even imagine.

- I have realized, I have seen in my own life, that you can create money and whatever else you want in a sane, balanced way — even in an easy and relaxed, healthy and positive way. Keep affirming this long enough, and it becomes true in our experience.

Act as if

It were impossible

To fail.

— **Dorothea Brand**
Wake Up and Live

LESSON 7

. . . .

LOVE CHANGE AND
LEARN TO DANCE

THE DAY THAT CHANGED MY LIFE

I've mentioned my thirtieth birthday several times. Let me now tell the story in some detail, for it contains within it clear examples of some of the most important keys in this Course. It was a day that changed my life, dramatically and unalterably. I woke up in a state of shock. I couldn't believe I was *thirty* already — I felt about twenty-one. But it was undeniable: I wasn't a kid anymore.

I was definitely not in the mood for a party or celebration of any kind — I knew I had some serious thinking to do. I spent most of the day prowling restlessly around my little apartment, thinking about my life — the good, the bad, and the ugly. I had always done what I loved — that was one key I knew from birth. I had been an actor, then a student of Zen and various other spiritual things, then a rock 'n roll musician. But the band had fallen apart, and several months passed where, when I now look back on it, I haven't the faintest idea what I did. Time just flew by.

I was unemployed, scrounging to come up with $65 a month for the rent on a little studio apartment in the slums.

I had no money. Worst of all, I had no direction. I had been fired as a busboy and dishwasher because I was too slow. I had a few temporary jobs, weeding gardens and — one of my least favorite activities — spraying and dusting all the plastic plants in a large apartment building. My life was cruising along like a ship on the ocean, but somebody had forgotten to chart a course.

Then I remembered a little game I had played one time about eight years before, during a short-lived back-to-the-land experiment. We were sitting around a fire and one couple said, "Let's play a game we played at church camp. Let's imagine five years have passed, and everything has gone as well as you can possibly imagine — what would your life look like?"

We all went around the circle and described our ideal scene. I don't remember a word I said — proof it had no effect in my life. I was given a great key to success, to fulfillment, but didn't see it, and had no idea what it could mean in my life — until the day I turned thirty, when I remembered the game and played it, by myself this time.

I asked myself, "What kind of life do you want, in five years? What is your ideal scene?"

The answer immediately sprang to mind:

"I want to write books and record music, and have a successful company that publishes them — and I want a beautiful white house on a hill in Marin County, and a peaceful, joyful family life."

As important as the words that came to mind were the images and feelings they carried: I had an image of a company that was like a great ship, carried along by its own momentum, and a feeling that it could actually be done in a way that was stress-free, in an easy and relaxed manner.

I remember that day so well, even though it was over twenty-five years ago. I remember my exact thoughts. As soon as I dared to dream my ideal scene, a huge wave of doubts and fears arose, all based on fear.

My inner critic or critical parent or whatever you want to call it leapt forward and said, forcefully, "That's *way* too much, Marc! Writing books and music, starting a business, dreaming of a big house — just *pick one thing,* and focus on that."

Our inner critic is usually so reasonable and intelligent. Part of me certainly felt that it was far better to focus on one thing at a time, but another part of me disagreed — the part of me that imagined the ideal scene — and I felt a passion for my new dream, a desire to go for the whole enchilada. I wanted it all and, not only that, I wanted it *in an easy and relaxed manner, in a healthy and positive way.*

My voices of inner resistance just laughed at that one. "Impossible!" they said, with vehemence. "You know when you start your own business you have to work sixty or eighty hours a week; you have to be totally absorbed in it; it has to be your *single burning obsession.* You can't have much of a life — you certainly can't write books and record music and run a company and have a family life and have time for yourself! Impossible! There aren't that many hours in the day! You'll be a jack-of-all-trades, and master of none!"

Most of my inner voices were absolutely convinced of this, and their arguments were convincing. But then I thought of something: Somewhere I had heard that Buckminster Fuller, the famous inventor of the geodesic dome and other things, decided to live his life as a scientific experiment, where he is the test subject as well as the experimenter.

So I said to all my inner doubts and fears, "Look, you're probably right. It's probably all an impossible pipe dream, I grant you that. There's very little chance I can do, be, and have everything I want in an easy and relaxed manner, in a healthy and positive way. But it's a nice dream, isn't it? It's certainly worth trying as a little experiment, even though it will probably fail — but what's lost if I just try it and fail? I won't be any worse off, and I'll certainly have learned something."

I ended up making a deal, a compromise with all my doubts and fears. I would make an experiment for a year or two. I would attempt to move toward my ideal scene, and I would do it my own lazy ex-rock musician way, easy and relaxed, and see if it worked. If it didn't work, I would abandon the project. Or try to do it in a different way.

Without fully realizing it consciously, I had stumbled on a great key:

KEY 102

Look at your life as an experiment.
Make a compromise with all your doubts and fears:
For a year or two, do what you can to move
toward your ideal scene, in an easy and relaxed manner,
in a healthy and positive way.
See what happens!

I remember thinking that my inner critic was probably right, and I would have to become more hardworking, more Type-A, if I was actually going to succeed in a business, or write a book, or record some music. But it was certainly a worthwhile experiment to try to do it in my ideal way, working when and only when I wanted to, with ease.

My inner critics were sure I would fail, but agreed to give me a year or two to try my hopelessly idealistic, ungrounded plan to build my castle in the air.

And so I went ahead with my dream and, on that day, I discovered all of the beginning steps in this Course: I wrote down my ideal scene, and realized it was filled with goals. I wrote down a list of my goals on a separate sheet of paper. There were about twelve of them in all.

I paced around my room and said each goal out loud, adding to each goal the powerful phrase I have mentioned so many times before, a phrase I had read in a book by Catherine Ponder: *In an easy and relaxed manner, in a healthy and positive way.... Sometimes I'd add, In its own perfect time, for the highest good of all....*

I put my ideal scene and goals into a folder, and I wrote on the outside of it: *I am now creating the life I want.* And I signed it with my name, in big letters.

I continued nearly every day to affirm my goals. Changes started to happen quickly, various plans came to mind, opportunities appeared — and best of all, I found my inner critic was totally wrong and my intuition was right. I found I could create success without becoming a slave to my work. I could always find a way to choose to do things in an easy and relaxed manner, in a healthy and positive way, in its own perfect time, for the highest good of all. In fact, I found it is the simplest and best way to do things in general, both short-term and long-term.

Now, more than twenty-five years later, I sometimes stroll around my big white house on the hill and say to myself, "Can it really be this easy? Can I really have a life that's this relaxed, with this much time to goof off and enjoy my family and my solitude?"

And the answer is obviously yes, because I've been doing it for years. But I am continually learning how to relax even more deeply with it all; I am always learning new things, of course, and life just gets easier and easier. My schedule is completely flexible, so I can relax and be lazy whenever I feel like it.

Life has become a dance, not a struggle. I believe the single most important thing I did and continue to do is to simply affirm, over and over, that I am reaching whatever it is I dream of *in an easy and relaxed manner, in a healthy and positive way, in its own perfect time, for the highest good of all.*

Once I started doing this regularly, my life changed dramatically. New opportunities appeared, everywhere. They had been there all along, but I had not prepared myself to even see them, much less take advantage of them.

HERE IS A KEY

Here is a key that affected me deeply; a phrase I've played over and over in my mind hundreds of times over several decades, especially during times of disappointment or anxiety. It is an important key, couched in an enigmatic little phrase, that I heard in San Francisco in the late sixties from a spiritual teacher named Satchidananda. I only heard him speak one time, but he gave me something I'll never forget.

He sat calmly in meditation as he talked, and he chuckled as he said,

KEY 103

*Make no appointments
and you'll have no disappointments.*

— Swami Satchidananda

We immediately say, *What?* — what about my appointment calendar? Isn't that an essential tool? It certainly is for me. The key, of course, is that he meant the *expectations* that come when we make our appointments. Have no expectations, and you'll have no disappointments.

I studied Buddhism for several years after that, and realized that little phrase summed up a great truth that Buddha taught — the first of his four "Noble Truths," or Great Truths — and it's still invaluable for all of us today: The world out there doesn't cause our disappointment. We cause our own frustration and disappointment, because we have *expectations* of how things should be. If we didn't have those expectations, we wouldn't be disappointed.

The cause of our suffering and anxiety is within us. And the cure is within us as well. That simplifies things immeasurably. And it's not impossible to change: There are all kinds of different ways to deal with our problems, different tools to help us do it. Many of them are in this Course.

Here's a key: We can learn to accept change, even to love change, by letting go of our expectations of how we think things should be. Once we learn to accept what is, we can learn to love it all — all of life, in all of its never-ending parade of changes.

LOVE CHANGE

A KEY I HEARD ON THE RADIO

I heard a newscast, years ago, that reported on PepsiCo's remarkable success and continued growth. It quoted the CEO of the giant company saying he had only three rules:

> *Love change, learn to dance,*   KEY 104
> *and leave J. Edgar Hoover behind.*

It was to those three things he attributed the remarkable ongoing growth of his huge corporation.

My first response was *love* change? Isn't that a lot to ask? In fact, isn't it nearly impossible at times? Even simply accepting change is a huge challenge. To love change you need to be enlightened.

But as I reflected on those words a bit, I realized that *loving change* is a wonderful goal, a great ideal to shoot for. Accepting change is one thing, but if we can learn to love change, we can learn to fully, completely love life. We can find what there is to love in every moment.

This is a great goal, a great challenge for all of us. One book helped me make a quantum leap in this area — a book I've mentioned repeatedly and highly recommend to everyone: Eckhart Tolle's *The Power of Now* (and/or *Practicing the Power of Now*). It is the best book I have ever read: It is clear and powerful, giving us what we need to change our lives and even our world *in this moment, now.* It can teach us to love change and learn to dance with everyone and everything that comes our way in life.

I have been reading *The Power of Now* every day for over two years. I pick it up nearly every morning and begin to read where I left off. For over eighteen months, I've been stuck on the bottom of page 155. Every day, I read the same sentence — the same great key to a life well lived — and I think, *I've got to remember this, every moment of the day.*

Throughout the day, the words often come back to me. It is a key I've pondered for a year and a half — who knows how much longer I'll have to keep reading the same page over and over, every day? It's well worth it, though — repeating this phrase so often has had a major impact in my life.

Here's the key — we've seen the beginning of it before (a drum roll would be nice here):

KEY 105

To offer no resistance to life
is to be in a state of grace, ease, and lightness.
This state is then no longer dependent on things
being in a certain way, good or bad.

· ·

Think about that for a while.

In the past six months or so, I have on occasion read beyond those sentences — and what he says next is another remarkable key:

> *It seems almost paradoxical,*   KEY 106
> *yet when your inner dependency on form is gone,*
> *the general conditions of your life,*
> *the outer forms, tend to improve greatly.*
> *Things, people, or conditions that you thought you*
> *needed for your happiness now come to you with no*
> *struggle or effort on your part, and you are free to enjoy*
> *and appreciate them — while they last.*
>
> *All those things, of course, will still pass away,*
> *cycles will come and go, but with dependency gone*
> *there is no fear of loss anymore.*
> *Life flows with ease.*
>
> *The happiness that is derived from*
> *some secondary source is never very deep.*
> *It is only a pale reflection of the joy of Being,*
> *the vibrant peace that you find within*
> *as you enter the state of nonresistance.*
>
> — Eckhart Tolle, *The Power of Now*

Everything we thought we needed to be happy is from a
secondary source, and it is only a pale reflection of the happiness, ease, and peace that we can discover within us. The
key to this discovery is to give up our resistance — to accept
change and learn to dance.

Isn't that what we all want, underneath it all: a life that
flows with ease?

It is perfectly attainable, and we don't even need to learn

to *love change* in order to get there. All we need to do is fully accept what is; all we need to do is to let go of any resistance we have to what is going on in the moment.

Nearly any child or animal or Zen master can show us how to do it. It doesn't involve doing anything except letting go. Let go and trust in the universe. The intelligence that guides animals, plants, and galaxies guides you too. Let go and realize that you are part of an abundant world, and things will work things out for the best. As they say in many Christian churches and Twelve-Step programs,

KEY 107   ***Let go and let God.***

Substitute any word or words you wish for "God." Let go and let the universe do its work — use your own words to describe your understanding of the process.

We don't need to — and in fact can't — control the circumstances of our lives. But we can accept those circumstances, and even embrace them, for they make each one of us completely unique, and give us the great challenges and opportunities we all have.

LEARN TO DANCE

A BEAUTIFUL IMAGE, A GREAT KEY

Our work, our play, our lives in their wholeness can be a dance instead of a struggle. Learn to dance with whatever life gives you. Learn to dance with your co-workers, your customers, your intimate partners, with *everyone* you meet.

Life can be a dance, not an ongoing parade of problems; business can be a dance, not a race or a struggle, when you apply some of the things you learn in this Course. Why not dance through life rather than battle through it? Dancing is a lot more fun than fighting — and it doesn't cause pain or leave scars.

The way we learn to dance with each other is by learning to live and work in partnership with each other.

When we dance together, we find win-win solutions.   KEY 108
This is a great key to lasting success.

In order to learn to dance, the step that follows is essential.

LEAVE J. EDGAR HOOVER BEHIND

DOMINATOR MANAGEMENT

J. Edgar Hoover was director of the FBI during World War II, the Cold War, and the Vietnam conflict. In these years, we reached the heights of the absurdity of the dominator model, and Hoover's management style was a product of its time: the epitome of "dominator-style management."

He was infamous for completely controlling his employees' actions. His management style was dictatorial; everything came from the top down; everyone was told exactly what to do and how to do it.

That management style, of course, creates endless conflict and complexities — and, worse yet from a business point of view, endless inefficiencies. One person on top can never know what is going on throughout the entire organization, much less be able to clearly direct every element at every level of that organization. It's an impossible, unwieldy structure.

PARTNERSHIP MANAGEMENT

Now there are options, thank God. We don't have to continue old habits, old models of behavior that aren't working anymore. The key is to move as far as possible toward the ideal of perfect partnership in our relations.

Partnership-style management is not only far more enjoyable, it's far more efficient. In our company, every employee is considered a manager — because every employee manages *something*. We work with all our managers to make sure their job and its goals are clear, and then we challenge them to do their job and reach those goals in their own way, with their own management style.

It's the kind of "hands-off" management policy that would drive J. Edgar Hoover into anxiety attacks, because it means letting go of control, and trusting that something bigger and better will emerge — which is exactly what happens.

Hire people who are passionate about their job, clearly define their responsibility, and let them do it in their own way. They're the ones in the trenches, after all, doing the work all day. They see what's going on, far more than any manager in some remote office. Give them a share of the profits they generate and watch them shine. They'll do their job far better than you could do it.

Instead of management from the top down, make it management from the bottom up. Let the employees tell management how best to do the job the employees were hired to do — and employees and management alike will excel in their performance.

Combine that level of freedom and responsibility with generous profit sharing, so employees get a significant share of the profits they generate, and you have a great key to success. Remember the great quote from H. S. M. Burns (in Lesson 5):

Treat your employees well, and you'll soar to greatness on their accomplishments.

Best of all, in my opinion — and also worth repeating — with the partnership management that we've established, I don't even have to be in the office for the business to run smoothly. Everyone is so empowered and responsible I can take all the time I want and need away from the workplace, and my company hums along.

I've heard so many employers over the years moan about how hard it is to find good people — that to me says far more about those employers than it does about people in general.

I've never had any problems finding good people, or keeping them. The world is full of good people — if they're treated with respect, and treated as adults. If you assume they're responsible, they act responsibly. If you challenge them, they rise to the challenge. There are a few exceptions, of course, but the vast majority of people you hire will do well in their work if you manage in partnership with them.

I've seen this happen, over and over, and I've said it before and I'll say it again:

> *Partnership management*   KEY 109
> *turns a mediocre employee into a good employee,*
> *a good employee into an excellent employee,*
> *and an excellent employee into a creative force*
> *who substantially contributes to the company's growth*
> *and excellence.*

Add any notes or quotes from this lesson that you particularly want to remember into your folder. Review it regularly.

SUMMARY

- Keys to your success are everywhere. Once you have begun the work in this Course, once you create your ideal scene and take at least the first few steps toward it, you'll notice you start to receive guidance from all kinds of sources.

- You may need to learn only a small fraction of the material in this Course before you reach the goals you have set for yourself. Along the way, you will certainly discover your own keys, and apply them in your own way.

- Here's a great key to happiness: The world out there doesn't cause our disappointments. We cause our own disappointment, because we have *expectations* of how our lives should be. If we didn't have those expectations, we wouldn't be disappointed.

- It is possible to learn to accept change, even to love change, but the only way we can do it is by letting go of our expectations of how we think things should be. We have to learn to accept what is before we can learn to love all of life, in its never-ending parade of changes.

- Our work, our play, our lives in their wholeness can be a dance instead of a struggle. Learn to dance with your co-workers, your customers, your intimate partners, with *everyone* you meet. Dancing in partnership is a lot more fun than fighting — and it doesn't cause pain or leave scars.

- Dancing together means letting go of all forms of domination and attempts to control others. The old dominator-style management creates endless conflict, complexities, and inefficiencies. Partnership is a far better alternative.

- Our greatest challenge as managers and creators is to move as far as possible toward the ideal of *partnership* in our relations. Partnership-style management is not only far more enjoyable, it's far more efficient.

- Instead of management from the top down, make it management from the bottom up. Let the employees tell management how best to do their jobs — and they'll excel in their performance. Combine that level of freedom and responsibility with generous profit sharing, so employees get a significant share of the profits they generate, and you have a great key to success.

- Partnership management turns a mediocre employee into a good employee, a good employee into an excellent employee, and an excellent employee into a creative force who substantially contributes to the company's growth and excellence.

In an easy and relaxed manner,

In a healthy and positive way,

In its own perfect time,

For the highest good of all. . . .

. . . .

DISCOVER YOUR CORE BELIEFS, AND LEARN HOW TO CHANGE THEM

WE ARE LIMITED ONLY BY OUR BELIEFS

We know the universe is vast, beyond our abilities to conceive. We can see how abundant nature is. Yet many of us believe that resources are scarce, and there isn't enough to go around.

This belief, like all others, is not true in itself, but becomes true in our experience if we believe it. And like all other beliefs, it can be changed. This is not a theory; a great many people have proven it can be done. I have changed my beliefs from scarcity to prosperity, so have countless others — and so can you.

> *We live in a limitless universe,*　　KEY 110
> *limited only by our beliefs.*

This is the same as saying that, in an abundant world, we are limited only by our *thoughts*. Beliefs are thoughts. Thoughts can change — in fact they change all the time. Usually the process is subconscious, but we can learn to *consciously* change our thoughts — as well as our underlying beliefs. When we do, we change our entire life experience.

THE CORE BELIEF PROCESS

The process of changing your beliefs is not difficult: All you need to do is answer a few questions with as much honesty as you can and then craft a few effective affirmations. But don't let the simplicity of the core belief process cause you to underestimate it. This is an extraordinary bit of knowledge that gives us a phenomenal power: the power to consciously change our beliefs and, as a result, change our world as well.

I've written about it before, and so has Shakti Gawain,[*] but it's one of those things we need to hear — and do — repeatedly before we get it on a deep, effective level. Once we get it, we have a powerful tool to help us create what we want in our lives.

KEY 111

*We can consciously choose to create
a more satisfying life experience.*

The process works best when you're upset about something, because then it's very easy to identify all your thoughts about the problem, all the tapes running through your head. But the process works very effectively too when you're not particularly upset yet have a problem you want to resolve.

Here are the steps of the process. It's good to sit down and take a deep breath and relax as much as you can before going through it.

---

[*] Shakti Gawain wrote about the core belief process in *The Creative Visualization Workbook* (New World Library, 1995), and some of the following is reprinted from her book.

THE CORE BELIEF PROCESS

1. THINK OF A PARTICULAR PROBLEM, SITUATION, OR AREA OF YOUR LIFE YOU WANT TO IMPROVE.

Describe it — take two or three minutes to think about it or talk about it in general.

2. WHAT EMOTIONS ARE YOU FEELING?

Name the specific emotion, such as fear, anger, frustration, guilt, sadness.... (At the risk of making a broad generalization, I have found most women usually do this very quickly, and sometimes men stumble around in their heads before they can bring their attention down into their bodies and simply describe their feelings.) Don't get into any particular thoughts you're having about it at this point, just pinpoint the single word that describes the emotion.

3. WHAT PHYSICAL SENSATIONS ARE YOU FEELING?

Explore your body, from your toes to the top of your head. Is there tension somewhere? What's going on in your stomach? What is your breathing like?

4. WHAT ARE YOU THINKING ABOUT?

What tapes are running in your head? What conditioning or programming can you identify? What negative thoughts, fears, or worries are you having? Take a few minutes to describe your thoughts.

5. WHAT IS THE WORST THING THAT COULD HAPPEN IN THIS SITUATION?

Ask yourself, What is my greatest fear in this situation? If your greatest fear came true, then what would be the worst thing that could happen? If that happened, what would be the very worst thing that could possibly happen?

These questions bring your deepest fears to light.

6. WHAT IS THE BEST THING THAT COULD HAPPEN?

What would you like to happen ideally? What is your ideal scene for this area of your life?

You may find this harder to express than your worst fears. If so, your fears may have been dominating and overwhelming your vision of success. Maybe you have been focusing more on the half of the glass that is empty than the half that is full in your life. Keep the best things, the best possibilities, in mind.

7. WHAT FEAR OR LIMITING BELIEF IS KEEPING YOU FROM CREATING WHAT YOU WANT IN THIS SITUATION?

Once you've explored this, write your limiting or negative belief in one short sentence, as simply and precisely as you can. If you have more than one, write them all down. Put them in the form of a belief: *I believe that I'm inadequate.... I believe it's hard to make money.... I believe my life is stressful and unhealthy at times....*

8. CREATE AN AFFIRMATION TO COUNTERACT AND CORRECT THE NEGATIVE, LIMITING BELIEF.

It should be short and simple and meaningful to you, in the present tense, as if it is already happening. *I am enough.... I am now creating abundance in my life.... I now live and achieve my goals in an easy and relaxed manner, a healthy and positive way....*

Your affirmation is the opposite of your core belief, turning a negative, limiting phrase into a positive, expansive one. Here are some examples:

LIMITING BELIEF: *I don't have enough time to do the things I want to do.*

AFFIRMATION: *I have plenty of time to do the things I want to do.*

LIMITING BELIEF: *I have to struggle to survive.*

AFFIRMATION: *I am creating total success in an easy and relaxed manner, a healthy and positive way.*

LIMITING BELIEF: *I'm under a lot of pressure at work; it's unavoidable in my high-pressure job.*

AFFIRMATION: *I now relax and enjoy myself at work, and accomplish everything easily.*

LIMITING BELIEF: *Money corrupts people.*

AFFIRMATION: *The more money that comes into my life, the more power I have to do good for myself, for others, and for the world.*

LIMITING BELIEF: *The world is a dangerous place.*

AFFIRMATION: *I now live in a safe, wonderful world.*

LIMITING BELIEF: *It's so hard to have a loving, ongoing relationship.*

AFFIRMATION: *I now have a loving, ongoing relationship, in an easy and relaxed manner, in a healthy and positive way.*

LIMITING BELIEF: *I don't have what it takes to succeed.*

AFFIRMATION: *I have everything I need to create success as I choose to define it.*

OR: *I am now creating my success, in an easy and relaxed manner, in a healthy and positive way.*

9. SAY OR WRITE YOUR AFFIRMATION REPEATEDLY, OVER A PERIOD OF SEVERAL DAYS.

Write your affirmation down and put it where you'll see it often. Repeat your affirmation silently to yourself, while relaxing. Picture everything working out exactly as you want it to.

Write it ten or twenty times a day, if necessary, until you feel you've absorbed it as a positive core belief. If negative thoughts come up, write those thoughts on the back of the paper, then keep writing the affirmations on the front until it feels free of any emotional resistance.

That's the entire core belief process. It has worked magic in my life. I'll give you a real-life example.

A TRUE EXAMPLE

In my previous book, *The Ten Percent Solution,* my old mentor Bernie took me through the core belief process. It was a fictionalized tale; the true story is that I went through the process alone, in my car, driving down the freeway. The process at that moment was a powerful experience for me, and I remember it clearly, though it was more than twenty years ago.

I'd had my business for five or six years, and I was still struggling. The limiting beliefs that *starting a business is stressful* and *life is a struggle* and *it's so hard to make money* were obviously dominant in my subconscious mind. Our little publishing company wasn't making any money, and we had set up another company to distribute our books that collapsed and went bankrupt, forcing us close to bankruptcy — and forcing most of the twenty-four other little publishers that were involved out of business, because the distribution company sold books for *six months* without paying any of us anything as it finally went belly up.

Life certainly looked and felt like a struggle. I had about $65,000 in credit card debt (and this was back in the early 1980s, when that was a much more significant amount of money). I didn't have the income to support my monthly "nut," as we called it: mostly rent and credit card payments. I kept going only because I was offered more and more credit cards, and I'd take the cash advances and use them to make the minimum payments on all the other cards. I felt like I was headed for disaster.

I remember one hour of one day so vividly: I was rushing down the freeway, heading for the nearest bank to make a cash withdrawal on a new credit card that had just been sent to me. I was frustrated and agitated — and realized it was a perfect time to do the core belief process, something I had fortunately learned about several years before. I went through it by myself, as I flew down the freeway.

"Okay, what's the problem?" I said out loud to myself, *"What situation in life do you want to improve?"*

I answered immediately and vehemently. "My financial situation! I'm sinking! I'm way too deep in credit-card debt. Someday the bottom will fall out," I said, aware that I was echoing a line from one of Bob Marley's great songs.

"What emotions are you feeling?"

"Fear, anger, frustration — definitely! Guilt." I took a breath deep into my heart. "Sadness, too."

"What physical sensations are you feeling?"

I took another deep breath. "There's a jittery anxiety in my stomach — my neck and shoulders are tight. My chest is tight. I feel kind of tired and drained."

"What are you thinking about? What tapes are running through your head?"

"I'm thinking I'm just out of control financially. I'm not capable of dealing with money — it's that simple — money is beyond me. I'm a fool with money. It's sand through my hands."

I went on for a while, beating myself up for being so stupid and conflicted and inept.

"What's the worst thing that could happen? What's your greatest fear?"

"Bankruptcy...failure."

"What if that happened? What's the worst that could happen?"

"Despair. Destitution."

"What if that happened? What's the very worst thing that could happen?"

"I would die a slow, painful death in the gutter, with no friends, no one around me, no one to care in the least."

(It's very good to examine our worst fears — when we do, we usually realize that the odds of them actually happening are extremely slim.)

"Now, what's the best thing that could happen? What is your ideal scene?"

I remember specifically that the best-case scenario was harder to imagine than the worst-case scenario, which had sprung to mind easily. The best-case scenario took me a while to envision.

"I seem to be incapable of saving regularly and budgeting my way out of debt, so the best thing that could happen is that my company has explosive growth, and I get big bonuses that completely pay off all debts and leave me with a large amount of cash for both saving and giving. I'd build a diversified portfolio that supports me for life, and give generously to friends, family, and organizations working for good. I'd save far more than ten percent of my income, and give away far more than ten percent as well.

"Ideally, everyone in my company becomes wealthy through profit sharing, and everyone is fulfilled as well, doing what they love to do. I become *a king in his generativity.*"

That was a phrase I'd heard from a friend who was quoting Robert Bly. It completely surprised me when it tumbled out of my mouth. I gave my ideal scene more thought, and got to other things that were more important:

"I have a life of ease, able to do what I want with my time...." That sure felt good to say — it even seemed to fill me with ease, at least for a moment, just by thinking of the word.

"And I contribute to the world, in a meaningful, substantial way, and help make the world a better place for all."

I was pleased with that ideal scene. It felt good to even just imagine it as a possibility.

"What fear or limiting belief is keeping you from creating what you want?"

I wrestled with this for a while. "I'm afraid I'm out of control. I'm afraid I'll fail. I'm afraid I don't have what it takes to succeed."

"Now put it in the form of a belief: What beliefs do you have?"

"I believe I'm out of control. I believe I don't have what it takes to succeed. I believe I'm heading for failure, maybe disaster."

"Now find an affirmation that completely counteracts those old limiting beliefs. What do you want to believe?"

"I want to believe I'm sensible and in control of my finances. I want to believe somehow I can be successful, financially and in every other way as well."

"Put it in the form of an affirmation, short and simple and in the present tense."

I thought about it, then these words came to mind:

I am sensible and in control of my finances.   KEY 112
I am creating total financial success,
in an easy and relaxed manner,
in a healthy and positive way,
in its own perfect time, for the highest good of all.

I had exited the freeway by this time, and I pulled over and wrote the words down on the back of a business card.

Just going through that brief process and writing those words made me feel better than I had felt in months. A great deal of my anxiety simply evaporated.

I went to the bank and withdrew the additional loan, but I told myself this wasn't going to happen again because I was sensible and in control of my finances and would soon pay off my debts.

Later that day, I wrote my affirmation on several different business cards and put one on my desk at work, right by the phone where I'd see it often, one in my billfold next to my cash, one on my dresser at home by my bed, one on the bathroom mirror. I kept that affirmation in front of me and repeated it often, especially when my anxieties would come up again.

A fascinating thing began to happen: My thought patterns began to change, and I began to see that in some ways I really was sensible and in control of my finances. I began to see that this whole arena of personal finances was not really all that complicated — it certainly isn't rocket science — and in fact there are just a few simple rules: You have to make more than you spend. (Duh!) You have to live within your means.

Another surprising thing began to happen: rather than feeling overwhelmed by my debt and all other the difficulties of a start-up business, I opened up in some way to seeing new possibilities. I began to see my ideal scene more clearly — what I wanted and needed to solve the problems in front of me — and new opportunities kept appearing that pointed me in the direction of success, in exactly the way I chose to define that success, in an easy and relaxed manner, in a healthy and positive way.

All this as a result of repeating that single affirmation, over and over: I am sensible and in control of my finances. I am creating total financial success.

It was my ideal scene, rather than the scenario of my

fears, that soon came into my life, exactly as I had affirmed it and hoped it would be.

Keep affirming your ideal scene, keep it in mind in whatever way you can, and soon you'll be stepping into it in reality.

Something of great value happens when you go through the core belief process: You let go of old beliefs and create new ones, let go of old thoughts and create new ones, and those new thoughts and beliefs have the power to tangibly affect your reality.

THE WATCHER

Another valuable thing inevitably happens when you go through the core belief process: You see how easy it is to stand back and observe your thoughts and feelings, and objectively describe them from a broader perspective. In doing this, you become aware of what is often called the *watcher.*

Just discovering the watcher is a valuable key in itself. Once you can take a good look at your agitation, or whatever else is going on, you realize there is more to you than those thoughts and emotions. There is a part of you that can stand back and observe — and that part of you is *not* agitated, that part of you is calm, clear, at ease.

Eckhart Tolle writes beautifully about it in *The Power of Now:*

When you listen to a thought, you are aware not only of the thought but also of yourself as the witness of the thought. A new dimension of consciousness has come in....

As you listen to the thought, you feel a conscious presence — your deeper self — behind or underneath the thought, as it were. This is the beginning of the end of involuntary and compulsive thinking.

Once we understand this, we understand the watcher. Eckhart Tolle goes on to take it a brilliant step further:

KEY 113

When you know you are not at peace,
your knowing creates a still space
that surrounds your nonpeace
in a loving and tender embrace
and then transmutes your nonpeace into peace.

— Eckhart Tolle, *The Power of Now*

It is our own awareness of ourselves — something each of us has and can quickly learn to recognize — that gives us the key to a life of grace, ease, and lightness.

A MINI-CORE BELIEF PROCESS

There will undoubtedly be times when doubts and fears arise. They're a natural part of every human life. Try this when it happens:

Look at your doubts and fears — and realize that just by looking at them, you have found the watcher, you've found a quieter place within that can simply observe, without judgment. Acknowledge all your doubts and fears — become aware of them and accept them. Put them into words. Then steer them into an affirmation. Work with those doubts and fears until you find the words that counteract them.

KEY 114

Once you clearly look at your doubts and fears,
you can clearly imagine their opposite,
and affirm that everything is now working out smoothly,
in an easy and relaxed manner,
in a healthy and positive way,
in its own perfect time, for the highest good of all.

Add any notes or quotes from this lesson that you particularly want to remember into your folder. (For years, I had the steps of the core belief process in my folder.)

SUMMARY

- We are limited only by our beliefs. This is the same as saying we are limited only by our thoughts.
- Our beliefs are not true in themselves, but they become true in our experience if we believe them.
- We can change our beliefs. Many of them naturally change and evolve throughout our lives, but we can also consciously change them. So why not change them for the better? *We can consciously choose to create a more satisfying life experience.*
- There is a simple process that helps us change our beliefs: the core belief process. It involves answering these questions — it is especially effective when we're in a difficult or stressful situation:

1. *What problem, situation, or area of your life do you want to improve?*
2. *What emotions are you feeling?*
3. *What physical sensations are you feeling?*
4. *What are you thinking about?*
5. *What is the worst thing that could happen in this situation?*
6. *What is the best thing that could happen?*
7. *What fear or limiting belief is keeping you from creating what you want in this situation?*
8. *Create an affirmation to counteract and correct the negative, limiting belief.*

9. *Say or write your affirmation repeatedly, over a period of several days.*

• When you go through this process, you discover many things, including "the watcher," the part of you that can quietly and calmly observe what is going on in your mind, without judgment, without reacting. Just discovering the watcher is a valuable key in itself.

• To do a mini-core belief process, just look at whatever doubt or fear has arisen within, observe it without judgment, and then find the affirmation that counteracts it *in an easy and relaxed manner, in a healthy and positive way, in its own perfect time, for the highest good of all.*

If you believe you can

— or —

If you believe you can't,

you're right.

— Henry Ford

· ·

Grow at Your Own Pace, with an Architecture of Abundance

Every business is a growth business; every career inevitably grows and evolves. Your business and career go through the same three stages that all living things go through: infancy, adolescence, and maturity.

INFANCY

When your business or career is in its infancy, you have to care for it constantly. You expect nothing of it, and have to support it completely. Care for your infant business or career as you would care for your infant child — with loving attention, with no expectation of any reward, being in the moment with it, accepting it as is, watching it grow, enjoying every step of the way.

Remember when you're in the infancy stage that later on you'll have wonderful, warm memories of this period. Just as parents have the stories they treasure about their children, you'll have your stories about the beginnings of your career or business. Enjoy this period as much as possible. Find the humor in it — there's a lot to laugh about.

This is true of all life, of course, and a great key to a life well lived: Laugh as much as possible. This phrase has become well known, and it's true: *Laughter is great medicine.*

Though you expect nothing from your infant business or career, you discover something wonderful along the way — the same thing you discover when you have a real infant in your home: As you give whatever you can and care for your infant, you discover deep feelings of a love like no other, a love that is absolute and unconditional. And that's only the frosting on the cake, because an endless stream of other benefits and blessings follow. You receive a great number of rewards as soon as you begin creating something you dream of deep within your soul.

You are a servant of your child, and you become a servant of your dream as well. Here's a great key to ponder, from the magnificent poet of India, Tagore:

KEY 116

> *I slept and dreamt that life was joy,*
> *I awoke and found that life was service.*
> *I acted and behold! Service became joy.*
>
> — **Rabindranath Tagore**

Your infant grows at its own pace; sometimes slowly, sometimes instantly, in a quantum leap. As James Allen says, *Be not impatient in delay, but wait as one who understands.* Your infant business or career will soon grow to adolescence.

ADOLESCENCE

An adolescent business or career can take care of itself, including the basic needs of its employees, but it certainly can't take care of its owners. In fact, the owners may still need to come in with some additional support if the adolescent stumbles for some reason, maybe because it's trying something unproven or risky or new.

Just as in raising a child, great patience is needed to build a successful business or career. Don't draw too much out of the company too fast. Keep retaining earnings in the company; keep saving personally.

Adolescents have voracious appetites — and they certainly can't be depended on to support their parents. They may need additional support well into maturity, especially if they're trying to do something innovative and creative.

ADULTHOOD

If you keep focusing on your dreams, and if you're patient and persistent, your company or career will grow into maturity and be able to support you and many others abundantly. Then and only then can you reap the rewards of the powerful combination of your vision and persistence.

You'll realize how much you have grown along with your business or career. You're a far different person overseeing and shepherding an adult business and career than you were when you were constantly feeding your infant business or career. You have matured; you've become wiser. You have expanded in many ways, mentally and emotionally. You have discovered some secrets that have made your success solid, tangible, and inevitable.

Then things really get fun. One of the most satisfying, enjoyable meetings we have every year is in January, when we look at the previous year's profits and decide what to do with them. This is certainly one of the greatest perks of a mature business.

A FORMULA FOR ONGOING SUCCESS

It took my company about five years to go through its infancy, and another five to go through adolescence. Even before it was profitable, we set up medical and dental care for all employees, paid for entirely by the company. Before it was profitable, I said to my employees, "Help me make a profit, and I'll share it abundantly with you."

Once we started making a profit, here's the formula we evolved for profit distribution. (We saw the general formula in Lesson 5; now we'll get more specific.) The exact percentages vary from year to year, depending on several factors — especially on the amount we need to retain in the company, because our accountant and bankers have their opinions about that, and we always listen to their input.

In general, our goal every year is this:

- We donate 5 percent of pre-tax profits to charity.
- One-third of the remaining 95 percent is retained in the company for growth and expansion.
- One-third is paid to employees — part of it as cash bonuses and the other part to fund their pension plans to the maximum amount allowable by law.
- One-third is given to owners.

The numbers are flexible and can change from year to year, depending on circumstances. It's an arrangement that works well for us.

PROFIT SHARING

I've said it before and I'll keep saying it until many more people put it into practice: Every company — whether making a profit or not — should have profit sharing with employees.

There are no exceptions to this rule, because it's one of the single best things you can do to build a company with an architecture of abundance.

As I've said, McDonald's should have profit sharing. The U.S. Postal Service should have profit sharing. Your company should have profit sharing. If you're an artist or someone else working independently, any assistants you have should have profit sharing — even if they only assist you part-time. It's for your own good — the employers and owners benefit as much or more than the employees, because the employees contribute so much to the bottom line. Believe me: This is not a theory. This has been proven over and over, in thousands of different companies.

Here's a simple way to put it:

Profit sharing unleashes a powerful creative force   KEY 117
that results in greater profits for everyone.

Profit sharing expands the pie of the profits so everyone gets a bigger piece. When you have profit sharing, you have the ingenuity of everyone working for the company, rather than the ingenuity of a relatively few people "at the top."

It's a great example of the power of partnership, and how it creates abundance for all.

ARE YOU A GARDENER OR AN ARCHITECT?

I've mentioned Kent Nerburn before: I love his writing — his books are the work of a great soul. He is also one of my closest and most perceptive friends.

One day he said to me, out of the blue, "Marc, you're a gardener, not an architect." That comment was food for thought, and it took me a while to understand what he meant. I came to see that, yes, there are many very different ways to build success, and some people are gardeners and some are architects.

Gardeners tend to grow things organically, planting tiny seeds and nurturing them into fullness with patience and persistence. Architects are able to draw up precise plans of whatever they intend to build; architects in the business world can build a great company by skillfully combining other pre-existing companies.

There are many, many different ways to achieve success. With the tools in this Course, you can design your own unique creation, whether you're a gardener or an architect, or both.

FULFILLING OUR PROMISE

We've mentioned *The Architecture of All Abundance* by Lenedra J. Carroll, the mother and manager of the highly successful singer, Jewel. It is a book worth reading and re-reading.

It was published in 2001, so I had already created the architecture of my abundance by the time I read it, but it's one of those rare books that, if I had read it twenty-some years ago, would have compressed my first five years of struggle into just a few years, or even just months, and helped me reach my goals far more quickly.

Everything happens in its own perfect time — I was obviously not ready for success in those first years. I had a lot working against me, all of it my own creation. I had a great many conflicting core beliefs that eroded my ability to create a foundation for my dream. I had a lot of inner work to do. But now much of that work has been done, and my work has become showing other people how to realize their dreams.

This Course and *The Architecture of All Abundance* can both help you take a quantum leap into a much higher level of success, if that's what you want. Both these books can show you how to create the success you want, as you choose to define it.

In the frontispiece of this book, we quoted some key questions from *The Architecture of All Abundance:*

What is a deeply satisfying human life, KEY 1
and how do we design one?
How do we share that information with each other?
What are we here to do together,
and what are we truly capable of
in the realm of human excellence?

These questions cut directly to what is essential in life: What is a deeply satisfying human life? Of course, there is a different answer for each different individual. What does having a satisfying life mean to you?

Once you've answered that, how do you design it for yourself? The answers to those questions lead to the essence of this Course.

The answers to these questions are not mysteries KEY 1
beyond our reach. CONT.
Fulfillment of the promise of our soul's nature is possible.
It is why we are here. It is our birthright.
The answers are found only in the inner frontiers of Being.

— Lenedra J. Carroll
The Architecture of All Abundance

The first chapter of *The Architecture of All Abundance* is titled "The Architecture of Stillness." It is only within us, in the inner frontiers of Being, that we find the source of our true success.

You've certainly seen that by now: In order to answer most of the questions in this Course, you have to look within and draw the words from the depths of your being. You've probably already discovered the essential need for some time of reflection, whether it means taking walks alone, meditating, exercising, doing yoga, gardening, washing dishes, or whatever else works for you.

Start within, in stillness. Then ask a question: *What does having a satisfying life mean to me? What do I dream of having? Of doing? Of being?*

Then wait for the answers to arise.

KEY 118   *Just by asking this question —*
What does having a satisfying life mean to me? —
we set boundless energies in motion
that put great mechanisms to work for us.

MAKE A DEAL WITH YOUR DOUBTS

As soon as you imagine your ideal scene, you are almost certainly in for a fascinating bit of "inner theater" — I know I was. I've written about it earlier: As soon as I dared to dream about what I really wanted in life, in an ideal world, a huge number of doubts arose, immediate and forceful, all based on fear.

I ended up, after much discussion with myself, making a deal with my doubts and fears. I talked my inner critics into a compromise, into letting me try this experiment: I would try for a year, maybe two at the most, to do it the way I really wanted to — to create my ideal scene in my ideal way, in an easy and relaxed manner, in a healthy and positive way. I genuinely felt that the end of a year or two I'd most likely end up agreeing with all my inner (and outer) critics and have to change my strategy and quit being lazy and become a Type-A workaholic, at least for a while.

I believed that was how the system worked: You had to work hard for your money.

My inner critics were absolutely sure I would fail in my foolish little experiment — after all, they firmly believe, they *know*, you've really got to work sixty to eighty hours a week to build a business. But they agreed to give me a year or two to try my hopelessly idealistic, ungrounded plan, to build my castle in the air, and try to do it in my own lazy way. They gave me a year or two to fail, to flop miserably, and come to the realization I had to work a lot harder in order to succeed in today's world.

The lazy part of me thought the experiment was a good idea because it allowed me to be as lazy as I wanted to be and not have to seriously get to work.

Nearly every morning I affirmed all my goals were now coming into being *in an easy and relaxed manner, in a healthy and positive way, in its own perfect time, for the highest good of all concerned.*

Within a year, there were all kinds of positive developments; within two years, I had no more doubt, and the inner critics were silenced. The process worked! Within two years, my start-up company was showing great promise, I had written a book and recorded an album of music. And, best of all, I was doing it in an easy and relaxed manner, in a healthy and positive way.

There were certainly times during those first years I worked hard — sometimes old beliefs take a long time to completely change. I got a full-time job as a typesetter, working five days a week from 4 P.M. to midnight. Those were good hours for me, because I had much of the day to work on my various projects. Sometimes I'd be writing my book or making new plans at 3 A.M.

It took many years for me to really understand the phrase, "Work smarter, not harder." It took many years until I found I could create the perfect work week for me, spending only about thirty hours at work, having thirty hours a week alone to myself, and spending about thirty hours a week with my family. (I'm counting the whole week, with weekends and evenings, and so we have about ninety waking hours on the average — a lot of time, when you think about it.)

It became clear to me that not only was it possible to work in an easy and relaxed manner, it was the sanest and most effective way to work in the long run. There is no burnout, stress is greatly reduced, and work and life in general are much more enjoyable. When you work this way, in other words, *you have a life.*

It's certainly worthwhile to try your own experiment. Give yourself a year or two, and move toward your ideal scene in every imaginable way, in an easy and relaxed manner, in a healthy and positive way.

Build in a lot of time for relaxation and rejuvenation. Take breaks when you feel like it. Allow yourself to be lazy at times. If you do, you'll find you have a lot more energy at other times.

It's the "Lazy Person's Guide to Success." Try it; you might like it. I saw this quote somewhere years ago. I may be paraphrasing, but it's a great key:

KEY 119

Of course we build our castles in the air.
That's where they should be.
Then we have to build a foundation under them.

— Henry David Thoreau

A SHORTCUT

Somewhere along the line, many years after I started working with these techniques, I found a shortcut. We've touched on this before, but it's worth revisiting, for this bit of advice can be tremendously helpful: It is likely that you don't need everything you think you need to fulfill your dreams.

When you imagine your ideal scene, when you list your goals, you are focusing your powerfully creative mind on doing, being, and having everything you want.

It can definitely be worthwhile to ask yourself afterward, What do I really want all that stuff for? What is the end result?

Find the answer in your own words. For most people, it has to do with a life of ease and happiness, fulfillment of some kind.

Now affirm that you have already achieved that end result. Find your own words; the affirmation may be something like:

> *I now have a life of ease and fulfillment.*   KEY 120
> *So be it. So it is!*

It might be much simpler than you think to create the kind of life you want. Affirm to yourself you're working smarter, not harder; go through some of the exercises in this Course and you will probably be able to find shortcuts in places you thought you'd have a long, laborious journey.

TAKE IT EASY

We hear and say it a lot, and it's one of the best pieces of advice around, when we stop and think about it:

> *Take it easy.*   KEY 121

Affirm you're doing things in an easy and relaxed manner — and soon you'll be doing more and more things in an easy and relaxed manner.

Through it all, remember to *take it easy.* That's great advice for all of us.

SUMMARY

- Every business, career, and life evolves through three stages: infancy, adolescence, and adulthood.
- When your business or career is in its infancy, you have to care for it constantly. You expect nothing of it, and have to support it completely.
- Your infant business or career grows at its own pace; sometimes slowly, sometimes instantly, in a quantum leap. As James Allen says, *"Be not impatient in delay, but wait as one who understands."* Your infant business or career will soon grow to adolescence.
- An adolescent business or career can take care of itself, including the basic needs of its employees, but it certainly can't take care of its owners — and the owners may still need to come in with some additional support if the adolescent stumbles for some reason.
- Don't draw too much out of an adolescent company too fast. Keep retaining earnings in the company; keep saving personally.
- If you keep focusing on your dreams, and if you're patient and persistent, your company or career will grow into maturity and be able to support you and many others abundantly. Then and only then can you reap the rewards of the powerful combination of your vision and persistence.

- Then things really get fun. One of the greatest perks of a mature business is profit sharing. Set it up so that employees share in the profits as much as the owners. This is a great key to ongoing success: Every company that makes a profit should have profit sharing with employees. There are no exceptions to this rule, because it's the single best thing you can do to build a company. *Profit sharing unleashes a powerful creative force that results in greater profits for everyone.*

- Build your success in your own unique way. Ask yourself: What is essential in my life? What makes it deeply satisfying? Then ask: How do I design it for myself? The answers will arise once you ask the question. Within your answers are keys to fulfillment.

- See if you can talk your doubts and fears into allowing you to make an experiment and try, for a year or two, to create your ideal scene, in an easy and relaxed manner, in a healthy and positive way. This is a worthwhile experiment — one that transformed my life.

- It is not only possible to work in an easy and relaxed manner, it is the sanest and most effective way to work in the long run: There is no burnout, stress is greatly reduced, and work and life in general are much more enjoyable. It's the lazy person's guide to success.

- It is likely that you don't need everything you think you need to fulfill your greatest dreams. Ask yourself, What do I really want all that stuff for? What is the end result? Begin with the end in mind, and you may find achieving that end is much simpler than you think.

- Great advice to remember: Take it easy.

- Find affirmations that work for you, and repeat them. Don't underestimate the power of words. They change our lives. Here are a few suggestions:

I now have a life of ease and lightness.

Every day, in every way,

I'm getting better and better.

I am working smarter, not harder.

I am now creating the life of my dreams,

In an easy and relaxed manner,

In a healthy and positive way,

In its own perfect time,

For the highest good of all.

LESSON 10

. . . .

GIVE ABUNDANTLY
AND REAP THE REWARDS:
THE TEN PERCENT SOLUTION FOR
PERSONAL AND GLOBAL PROBLEMS

THE TEN PERCENT SOLUTION

You've certainly heard at least parts of this key before — many, many times. Like every key in this Course, it bears repeating until it has an impact in our lives — and even after that. It bears repeating until we have transformed our lives and our world into our ideal scene.

The Ten Percent Solution is a simple program to understand, and a challenging one to implement. Don't let its simplicity fool you. Within it are keys to lasting wealth and — even more important — *personal fulfillment.*

There are three basic parts to it:

1
SAVE AT LEAST 10 PERCENT

This is a simple, practical, and *highly effective* way to create lasting wealth: *Save at least 10 percent of your income.* Start now. Even if you're in debt — start saving to first pay off that debt and then to build for your future.

If you have your own business and have at least a few employees, set up a profit-sharing pension plan like the one we have, where the company gives out substantial profit sharing every year, partly in cash and partly invested into a diversified portfolio for each employee in their retirement accounts. This way everyone automatically saves over 10 percent, and it costs them nothing.

Do whatever you can at work, then supplement it as much as you can. Saving 10 percent is excellent; saving 20 percent is even better. Set up a savings account and deposit at least 10 percent of every check you receive into that account for long-term savings. If you don't think it's possible, try it anyway. When you do it, you send a strong message to your powerful subconscious mind that you're going to live on 90 percent of your income. And in a short time, you find yourself doing just that.

KEY 123   *Saving 10 percent leads to*
financial independence.

It's so simple, yet so few do it. *Spend less than you make.* It's pretty obvious, isn't it?

Why don't more of us do it? As soon as we start saving regularly, we make an expansive mental and emotional shift. We realize in a deeper way that we live in an abundant world, and we see how we can easily and effortlessly tap into that abundance, that prosperity.

It's as easy as saving 10 percent. Saving more is even better. A woman I met at a seminar told me she was saving 70 percent of the income she was making as an exotic dancer. She was more than halfway through her plan of dancing for five years, and in two more years she would be set for life, able to support herself and her two children on the interest and rental income her investments make. She has her plan, and is implementing it.

LOWERING THE GRADIENT

If you can't save 10 percent, there's a great psychological trick called "lowering the gradient": Save 5 percent, or 3 percent. Start with 1 percent, if you have to — certainly you can save *one* dollar for every hundred that flows through your hands. Then move it up to three, then five, until you work up to ten.

I set aside 10 percent of every check that comes in. What has been even more helpful to me is visualizing and even praying for large chunks of cash to come in at times, and saving a much larger percentage of that — 50 percent or more. I have reached what radio show host Bob Brinker calls "critical mass" — I have enough in passive income from a variety of sources (mostly stocks, bonds, real estate) that I could happily live on that income without needing to work for a living.* (I continue to work, though, because I love my job!)

If you save just 10 percent, it will quickly grow into a substantial amount of money. Then the magic of compound interest occurs, and that money begins to make money on its own. You are now making money absolutely effortlessly.

Save just 10 percent, and you'll become a magician with money.

---

* Bob Brinker hosts a show on radio stations around the country (KGO in San Francisco) called "Moneytalk." It's filled with excellent nuts-and-bolts financial advice. Website: WWW.BOBBRINKER.COM.

2
GIVE AWAY AT LEAST 10 PERCENT

Here's another key, one that creates great solutions in the world — one we've all heard many, many times as well: Give away at least 10 percent of your income. Discover the power of *tithing* — giving 10 percent has great effects in both your own life and in the world.

I'm not sure who Charles Colton was — apparently he was a writer; I've never read his work. But a great visionary quote of his is floating around:

KEY 124

> *If universal charity prevailed,*
> *Earth would be a heaven, and hell a fable.*
>
> — **Charles Colton**

Those are wise words. If we all practiced charity, Earth would be a heaven. To the degree that more and more of us start to tithe and support various worthwhile organizations working for some good cause, the world becomes more and more a world that works for all its inhabitants.

If you have problems giving away 10 percent, lower the gradient again: Give away 5 percent, or 3 percent. Or *one*. Then steadily move back up the gradient, until you reach 10 percent.

The easiest way to make sure you do it is to set up another bank account and deposit 10 percent of your income into it. Use it only for donations. Your savings account tithes to yourself; with your donation account you tithe to the world.

Just watch, as soon as you set up clearly in your mind that this is a priority in your life (and setting up separate accounts for saving and for donations is a great help), you'll find you're quite capable of living on 80 percent of your income. You might have a few slips until you really get it, deep within, but you've clearly told your subconscious mind that saving and giving are priorities in your life — you want to save at least 10 percent and give at least 10 percent, and you *intend* to do it. Your subconscious says *Yes,* and shows you exactly how to do it, easily and effortlessly.

THE POWER OF GENEROSITY

This simple act of giving 10 percent (or more) shows us the power of generosity: By being generous, we create a dynamic set of solutions to the problems in our lives and our world. Generosity contains the power to *generate* — in fact, the two words have the same root word (*genus,* in Latin, to grow, to create family). To be generous is to generate endless creative energy, energy that comes back and supports you and affects your life in countless ways.

> *Giving at least 10 percent*   KEY 125
> *changes your life and your world for the better.*

Again I'll repeat: These words are not theory. It has been proven over and over throughout history that when these words are applied in people's lives, their lives change dramatically. These are words that help us in our evolution.

3
LIVE AND WORK IN PARTNERSHIP

Originally, what I called the Ten Percent Solution only had two steps: saving and tithing. But something felt incomplete about it, and I realized that people could save and tithe and still be part of the problem rather than the solution if they didn't do something else: work in partnership with one another.

KEY 126

The greatest solution of all is
to live and work in partnership
with yourself, your family and friends,
your work and community, your nation,
your world, nature, and spirit.

We dealt extensively with this key in Lesson 5. As soon as someone does any one of these three things — saving, tithing, and working in partnership — they're part of the solution. When someone does all three, they're a creative force for great and positive change in their life and in the world.

PARTNERSHIP CREATES SOLUTIONS

What if a great number of us brainstormed far more often on possible solutions to the problems in our world? What if it included listing at least twelve *What Ifs* about the next 10 or 50 or 100 years of life on Earth?

Many people are already doing this kind of work, and as their ideas enter into the mainstream — which is happening as I write this, and as you read this — we're seeing great change, quantum leaps in our evolution.

It's already begun. The twenty-first century will be one of great change. It's completely up to us whether that change will be for good or ill. This much is obvious to me and many others:

KEY 127

A partnership of corporations, governments,
nonprofits, and individuals can save the world.

Years ago, walking through the hills, I had a fascinating brainstorming session with myself, and saw a possible future for us and the generations to follow. It grew into a fantasy that kept recurring, and getting more detailed — and then I saw that it's not only possible, but it's already beginning to occur, around the world.

The way I first imagined it, the future unfolded almost like a Utopian novel. *What if:*

What if a nonprofit foundation was founded and grew to a huge size, big enough to fulfill its purpose, which is to get at least (1) 10 percent of the people of the world to give away at least 10 percent of their income; (2) 10 percent of the wealthiest people in the world to give away at least 10 percent of their assets; and (3) 10 percent of the corporations of the world to give away at least 5 percent of their pretax profits. This would be enough money to help everyone on Earth, on every level of society, to improve their lives. This would be enough to change the world.

It has already started with grassroot organizations, with people who are forming "Giving Circles," with wealthy individuals who are giving generously, and with corporations already donating part of their profits. It has already started within nonprofit corporations, and it has always been a major concern of governments and churches. The infrastructure is already being built. It just needs far more support, both with money and volunteers.

What if a single nonprofit or group of nonprofits and visionary people working together generate huge sums of money and mobilize a vast army of volunteers who do the work necessary to help everyone improve the quality of their lives? What if we had enough vision and resources so that the *entire global population* could move higher up the pyramid of human consciousness that was first formulated by the famous psychologist Abraham Maslow:

SELF-ACTUALIZATION:
FULFILLMENT OF PURPOSE
FULFILLMENT OF ARTISTIC OR BUSINESS OR HUMANITARIAN DREAMS

EDUCATION

THERAPY
TREATMENT, RECOVERY

SECURITY

FOOD AND SHELTER

We need to fuel more money and resources into helping people on the bottom levels of our society. With the support of enough people and corporations, we can certainly feed the hungry and house the homeless. We have the capability to provide free medical care for all, and recovery and therapy programs for those who need it.

Once we are fed and sheltered and healthy, we naturally move up the pyramid and become hungry for an education. Certainly we have the resources — when we work in partnership with our schools, communities, corporations, and governments — to provide free public education, from preschool and day care for infants up through graduate school. We have the resources to vastly improve our educational systems, including substantial pay raises for teachers on every level, so that they become what teachers should be in every society: respected, well-paid professionals doing critically important work.

Once we have an education, we're at the top of the pyramid, and we're ready to fulfill our artistic dreams, or business plans, or do humanitarian work. At this level, too, we need financing, support, and mentoring. What if we had art centers, business schools, and millions of other nonprofits and individuals that supported all of us in financing our dreams? And when people achieve their dreams, what if they all donate back to the organizations that supported them along the way, so that vast income streams are generated from those who have benefited as well as from outside contributors.

It's all doable. Our nonprofits, corporations, and governments together can generate enough money and people power to solve our global problems of hunger, homelessness, lack of medical care, lack of recovery tools and therapy, lack of good education, and lack of programs that support budding artists, entrepreneurs, and humanitarians.

The basic infrastructure is already in place, and we are building more and expanding daily. We are on the verge of a great international quantum leap — something that, as Barbara Marx Hubbard reminds us, will happen very quickly, in a burst of new ideas catching flame throughout the world. This will help us make that leap:

> *Donate at least ten percent of your income*   KEY 128
> *to groups and individuals working*
> *to improve the world.*
> *And encourage others in the businesses*
> *and communities around you to donate as well.*

When we give generously we reap countless rewards in our lives. One of the great rewards is that we begin to see solutions, everywhere, to what were formerly intractable problems.

A CHALLENGE TO US ALL

Let's challenge ourselves to be part of the solution rather than part of the problem. To do this, we need to first clearly imagine what the solutions are. Let's all imagine, each in our own way, how our lives and our world can improve. Let's imagine an *ideal scene* for the whole world. And let's take some steps forward, in whatever ways we can, toward that ideal.

This Course is filled with possibilities: Take some of these possibilities and run with them, or come up with some solutions of your own.

Add any notes or quotes from this lesson that you particularly want to remember into your folder. Review it regularly.

SUMMARY

- The Ten Percent Solution is a simple program to follow: Don't let its simplicity fool you. Within it are keys to lasting wealth and — even more important — *personal fulfillment*. There are three basic parts to it:

- 1. Save at least 10 percent of your income. This is a simple, practical, highly effective way to create lasting wealth. Save 10 percent or more, and you'll become a magician with money.

- 2. Give away at least 10 percent of your income. Discover the power of tithing — giving 10 percent has great effects in both your own life and in the world. As Charles Colton said, *If universal charity prevailed, Earth would be a heaven, and hell a fable.* As soon as you set up clearly in your mind that saving and giving are priorities in your life — and setting up separate accounts for saving and for donations is a great help — you'll find you're quite capable of living on

80 percent of your income. This simple act of giving 10 percent shows us the power of generosity: By being generous, we create an endless stream of solutions to the problems in our lives and our world.

- 3. The third part of the solution is to live and work in partnership with yourself, your family and friends, your work and community, your nation, your world, nature, and spirit.

- As soon as you do any one of these three things — saving, tithing, and working in partnership — you are part of the solution. When you do all three, you become a creative force for great and positive change in your life and in the world.

- Partnership creates solutions. A great many people are already living and working in partnership — and as soon as their ideas enter into the mainstream, we'll be seeing great change, quantum leaps in our evolution.

- A partnership of corporations, governments, nonprofits, and individuals can save the world. It's all doable. Our nonprofits, corporations, and governments together can generate enough money and people power to solve our global problems of hunger, homelessness, lack of medical care, lack of recovery tools and therapy, lack of good education, and lack of programs that support budding artists, entrepreneurs, and humanitarians.

- It has already begun. The infrastructure is already being built. It just needs far more support, both with money and volunteers. We all have the power to be part of the solution rather than part of the problem.

- This Course is filled with possibilities: Take some of these possibilities and run with them, or come up with something of your own.

If universal charity prevailed,

Earth would be a Heaven,

and

Hell a fable.

— Charles Colton

. . . .

BECOME MORE AWARE OF THE SPIRITUAL SIDE OF LIFE, THE POWER OF PRAYER, MEDITATION, AND RELAXATION

OUR PHYSICAL AND SPIRITUAL BODIES

It is easy to see how extraordinary our physical bodies are — a simple blade of grass is phenomenal, when we think about it. It grows, it generates more of its kind, it dies, the elements that formed it change into something else and become a new form in an eternal process of creation and destruction.

It is not so easy to see or understand the force that is behind all these living things. What animates a blade of grass?

We know that every DNA molecule contains a library of information, the complete building plans for the living thing it creates — but what power made those plans, and carries out the plans? How do we understand or describe the force that is capable of creating life as we know it?

We know how subatomic particles act and react, but what is the force that brings them together into ever more complex patterns of partnership that eventually result in a human being, or a tree, or a cricket playing its music?

Many of us have witnessed someone dying. One moment, they are the animated individuals we know them to be, the next moment they are gone, and we are left with a lifeless lump of material that we know has no connection anymore with the person we knew and loved.

What has left us?

Spirit has left — the vital part of us that animates us, and that moves on to other worlds after our death, living forever.

Call it what you will: spirit, soul, life, life energy, higher power, the Tao, the Great Spirit, the Force. I heard someone put it this way in an AA meeting:

KEY 129

> *If you don't believe in a higher power,*
> *go make a blade of grass.*

DISCLAIMER REPEATED

As I've said earlier, it isn't necessary to accept my beliefs as your beliefs in order to make these tools work for you. It isn't necessary to be a spiritual person, whatever that means for you, or even to believe in the existence of spirit. The tools in this Course will work for you as soon as you understand them in words that are clear and acceptable to you and you apply them in your life.

We've already seen an example earlier of a completely nonspiritual way to use these tools: Simply write your goals, every morning, over and over for a length of time. That little activity alone is enough to move you toward your goals.

Since childhood, I've been fascinated by the spiritual, and so it is a fundamental part of this Course. But if you can't or don't want to relate to this spiritual stuff, just skim or skip this part, and any other parts you want to skip.

KEY 130

> *Take what you need, and leave the rest.*
> *Find the tools that work for you,*
> *and use them.*

A NEAR-DEATH EXPERIENCE

There are many people who, for many reasons, deny that spirit or a spiritual level of being exists. You can't measure it in any known scientific way, after all, and it seems impossible to even sense, much less understand, things that are beyond the five senses of the body. Many people are skeptical of all things spiritual, and believe death is the end of it all, and nothing continues after the life of our physical bodies.

I don't know who it was that said that any new breakthrough ideas and great truths that come along are first laughed at, then resisted (sometimes violently), and then accepted as obvious truth. These truths may be scientific — look at how Galileo was persecuted for his beliefs — or spiritual — look at Jesus.

Many times it takes some kind of crisis to change our ideas and beliefs, like the death of a loved one or a near-death experience. At those times, our beliefs can change suddenly and dramatically.

It happened to me: I had two near-death experiences in my early twenties. I was an actor in a play called *Faust* — an original adaptation of the Faust legend in which Faust encounters the four enemies to the "man of knowledge" that Carlos Castenada described in *The Teachings of Don Juan* — ignorance, fear, pride, old age. Everyone in the cast — men and women — played Faust at different times, and I played him in a scene where I was persecuted for my scientific discoveries, and an angry crowd took me up to a platform high off the ground, put nooses around an arm, a leg, and my neck, and threw me off the platform, where I hung suspended in the air through the next scene.

I'd always catch the impact of the fall on my arm and leg, but something else happened the last two times I did it. Apparently I was caught by my neck first, right in the windpipe, because I immediately stopped breathing and lost all consciousness of my physical body. Both nights I had an identical experience:

Instead of feeling the impact of the ropes on my arm and leg, I was suddenly soaring along, sailing at great speed over beautiful green hills dotted with oak trees, like a scene from Tolkien, or the foothills of northern California. It was exhilarating.

I looked around to where I expected my arm and shoulder to be, and realized I didn't have a physical body at all — and yet I was fully, wonderfully conscious. I was aware of my surroundings and my thoughts and feelings. I was continuing on, purely in thought, feeling, and spirit, leaving my physical body far behind. It was ecstatic.

The experience went on and on; it was absolutely as real as the experience I'm having right now as I sit here writing this — yet it was far more vivid and alive and memorable. It was undeniable proof to me of the existence of a spirit within that is far beyond our physical, emotional, and mental bodies or states of being.

Call that spirit what you will — and there is no need to argue about what we choose to name it. Eckhart Tolle simply calls it *presence* or *being,* and leaves it at that. You can call it consciousness, or awareness. Or spirit, or life. Or God. Or Christ consciousness. Or the Tao. Or Buddha mind, the awakened state, cosmic consciousness, or our spiritual nature. Or the Great Spirit, or the Universe. Or the Source, or reality, or Ultimate Reality, or the quantum field, or the field of all possibilities. Or a new phrase I heard recently: the Mother Wave. Or some other word of your choice.

It is beyond any label we can give it, because it is beyond thought, and beyond our thinking mind's ability to express in words. In fact we need to go beyond thought to discover it. Great art can do it, being in nature can do it: shock us into mental stillness, so we can feel the spirit pouring through. Meditation can do it, being still and simply letting our thoughts go as they arise.

Who would have thought that the solution to so many of our problems is beyond thought?

The way we discover the spirit   KEY 131
is through cessation of thought —
then spirit shines through everything,
every molecule of the universe.

When we experience it directly, it is a wonderful thing. The fear of death weakens to a shadow of its former self. We realize that life in this physical body is but one brief stage of an endless and truly marvelous journey.

We realize we are far greater beings than we previously thought. We understand ourselves more completely, for we have a definite experience of all four levels of our being: physical, emotional, mental, and spirit.

Out of my body, I had a wonderful journey in spirit to worlds of spirit. It ended when I flew through a tunnel that was like a whirling funnel, and broke through a brilliantly shining light at the end — and was gazing into the face of the director of the play. He had noticed I was jerking spastically, and ran and got a ladder, climbed up and held me out of the ropes, then carried me down over his shoulder. (Thanks, Marlow Hotchkiss, for saving my life.) The play was so unusual the audience didn't even know it wasn't a normal part of the production, and it continued on. I laid on the floor. At first I didn't want to come back to this life. I wanted to continue the journey. It felt like I had been through graduate school, and had to come back and start over in kindergarten.

I had already played that role about fifty times with no injury, so I did it again the next night, and had exactly the same experience. From then on, the director took over the role, and managed to be thrown into the ropes without nearly dying.

OUR FOUR LEVELS OF BEING

In those two near-death episodes, I had direct experience of a consciousness — of *life* — beyond my physical body. Let's reflect on this awhile; there are some great keys to be discovered here — keys that can be life-altering.

It's very good to ask this question: *Who am I?*

You can put it this way as well: *What am I?*

When we begin to answer that question, we see right away that we're vastly complex, multifaceted beings. We realize — just as many spiritual traditions have taught for millennia, and science has taught for hundreds of years — that we have separate arenas of experience, distinct and different levels of being that can be described as separate bodies.

Each is a world unto itself. An ancient chant in Romany, the language of the Gypsies, gives us this key to understanding the nature of reality, of who we are:

KEY 132   *Many earths on earth there be.*

You could say it this way: There are many realities on Earth. During the course of our lives, we move through many very different worlds, and through different levels of being. Whether consciously or subconsciously, as we grow we try on different personas in different realities, and pick the ones we're comfortable with.

We've all experienced each of these different levels of

being, though we tend to specialize in one or the other, and sometimes we try to avoid one or the other, or even deny it exists.

1. OUR PHYSICAL BODY. We each have a truly phenomenal physical body that grows from the union of two tiny cells, a sperm and an egg. Within those cells are complex DNA molecules that contain the instructions to build tiny biological nano-machines that in turn build the intricate systems that create and preserve this marvelous body.

We can easily see and feel this body. We are fully aware of it, at least in some ways much of the time. It feels solid; it seems we can easily perceive it, though it is actually in a constant state of flux, repairing and changing all the time. It seems quite separate from the other things around us, though scientists tell us that on a molecular level there is no definite boundary between the outer layer of our skin and the so-called outer world.

Einstein once wrote, "There are two ways to view the world: One is that there are no miracles, the other is that everything is a miracle. I choose the latter." When we take an in-depth view of our physical bodies, it is obvious that they are miracles of creation.

2. OUR EMOTIONAL BODY. We all have a rich emotional life in addition to our purely physical existence. Sometimes our emotions completely dominate our consciousness. Some of us live on emotional levels of being almost exclusively — we're carried along from one strong current of feeling to another, and our so-called outside world is vastly affected by our emotional states.

Within our emotional body we can hold a lot of pain — so much that, as Eckhart Tolle points out, we create a "pain body" that can dominate us and overwhelm us. Many people identify so strongly with their pain body they mistake it for who they really are, and it runs their lives. They don't even realize there are other levels of being, some of them capable of calmly watching the play of emotions from a different level of consciousness.

In other words, we are greater than our emotional life, just as we are greater than our physical body and our mental capabilities. We can go beyond our body, our emotions, and our mind and quietly observe them from another level of being.

Our emotional body is much more than a body of pain, of course. We all experience a vast range of emotions, including love and joy as well as anger and fear. And within these currents of feeling in our body is the gateway to our intuition and to a life well lived.

We are all psychic, to some degree. We just need to tune in to our emotions, our feelings, for a wealth of intuitive knowledge and psychic information. It is always there, within us, waiting to be discovered. It has a still, small voice, and once we learn to listen to it, it will answer any questions we ask.

3. OUR MENTAL BODY. We have amazing mental capabilities, a great life and unique world that is exclusively of the mind. We have evolved a tremendous cerebral cortex with abilities we have only dimly begun to realize. The mind is limitless, infinitely expansive, able to penetrate the far mysteries of the known universe, able to probe beyond what is known.

A great many people in our culture are predominantly in this mental body, most of the time. Most of our formal education is exclusively mental. Most of us have a constant stream of words going through our consciousness, an endless mental commentary. Sometimes it's enough to give us a headache.

Eckhart Tolle mentions the crazy people in our cities

who go down the street yelling or muttering constantly. He says most of us are just like those people, except we keep our mouths shut. We still have a constant stream of thoughts — and many of us completely identify with those thoughts, and think that's who we are. We find something truly amazing and wonderful happens when we learn to find the "off" key that can quiet those thoughts, even if for just a few moments.

The great English writer John Milton suggested we look at it this way:

> *The mind is its own place, and can create*   KEY 133
> *a heaven of hell, a hell of heaven.*

If we can understand that, we can create a heaven on Earth. The mind is a wonderful tool, a great servant, but not a good master. The mind needs to be guided by the spirit. Once it is, it is limitlessly powerful.

4. OUR SPIRITUAL BODY. We all have a life of the spirit. We know it as children; we know it as we approach death. Many of us forget it in between. And yet it is the greatest part of who we are. It is the most expansive part of us, the highest, the most rewarding, the subtlest, the brightest, the most elusive, the most wonderful. It is the source of a peace beyond description, a peace that knows no opposite.

> *We are beings of spirit.*   KEY 134
> *It is the part of us that never dies.*
> *We are beings of light who live forever.*

Pierre Teilhard de Chardin put it brilliantly: We aren't physical beings who may have an occasional spiritual experience, we are spiritual beings having a physical experience.

If we can understand that, it puts every moment of our lives in a much greater perspective.

Take a moment to relax. Let all thought go for a moment and try to see, feel, sense, grasp, understand your spiritual nature.

Stop thinking for a moment. Close your eyes and meet your spirit. It is your presence, your being. It is your life energy.

When we consciously enter the vast body of our spirit, we understand the great truth behind all religions — we understand the "gospel," which means "the good news": We are spiritual beings who live forever. We are filled with an energy, a presence, that animates us and that lives eternally. We see that we truly are One with All, ultimately, a perfect part of the endless quantum field.

The key to this understanding is within us: *The Kingdom of Heaven is within.* It is our essential nature. We are an essential part of the all knowing, all powerful, and omnipresent source of creation.

Prayer and meditation give us access to this reality. Through prayer, we invite spirit into our physical, emotional, and mental lives. Through meditation, we can directly experience our spiritual nature, our oneness with all of creation, the truth of who we really are. For in reality we are directly connected, always and eternally, to the source of the creation of all. When we ask that source for guidance, we receive it.

KEY 135
Spirit is always waiting to answer your prayer.
Ask and you shall receive.

This is the power of prayer.

THE POWER OF PRAYER

We discover a great key once we understand our spiritual nature. It is a key not only to tangible, worldly success, but also to something far more important, a key to what is most important in life for all of us, in whatever words we want to use — fulfillment, contentment, self-realization, self-actualization, serenity, enlightenment, peace. Find the word that's best for you.

> *The spiritual path is simple,*   KEY 136
> *direct, and greatly rewarding.*
> *Ask in prayer, and let God work out the details.*

One of India's greatest contributions to the world is its vast body of ancient spiritual literature. The most accessible work that I have found so far is *The Bhagavad Gita,* or "The Divine Song."*

This great book gives us the story of the Divine Krishna talking to the very human Arjuna as they are poised on the field, preparing to fight the greatest battle of Arjuna's life. Krishna speaks with the gentle and powerful voice of Divinity, and gives us clear, transcendent instructions for a life well lived, and for full realization of the eternal wonder of who we really are. The key is to live a spiritual life — to have an awareness of our spiritual being, and to let that guide us at all times. The key is to remember that God (or spirit, or what-ever word we choose) is all knowing, all powerful, and om-nipresent, within every atom of the universe — including ourselves.

---

* The clearest version of *The Bhagavad Gita* that I've found is the beau-tiful prose version by Jack Hawley, *The Bhagavad Gita: A Walkthrough for Westerners* (New World Library, 2000).

When we call upon God, when we realize the presence of God within us, in whatever way we understand God, we avail ourselves of the creative forces of the universe.

KEY 137

When we pray,
we set in motion the ever-mysterious forces
that create the answers to our prayers.

The Bhagavad Gita goes into this in fascinating detail. It says, for example, there are four types of people on the spiritual path:

1. Those who are world weary or ill physically or disturbed mentally. The Gita nonchalantly says that the spiritual path will inevitably help these people receive what they want and need in life. If they ask, they will receive.
2. Those who are dissatisfied and wish to improve their lot in life, those who want more prosperity or satisfaction or fulfillment. Here too, the Gita says that the spiritual path works perfectly for those wanting to improve their lives.
3. Those who realize that the spiritual path is far more valuable than anything else in life, and seek a life of the spirit. They too will be guided by spirit to realize who they are. If they seek, they will find. They will attain self-realization, an awareness of their eternal connection to the Divine.
4. Finally, there are those who have already attained a state of constant awareness and realization of their spiritual nature. These people seek nothing, and need nothing. They have realized the reality of our spiritual nature.

The Gita states the truth so simply and clearly and emphatically it is downright blunt. We can put it this way:

If we pray, our prayers will be granted. KEY 138
If we seek to be guided by spirit,
we will be guided by spirit,
and everything else in our lives
will fall into place perfectly.

THE POWER OF RITUAL

It is a very good practice to start the day with a ritual of some kind that acknowledges and remembers your spirit. It's good to have an afternoon or evening ritual as well. And it's good to have something that reminds you to acknowledge spirit many times throughout your day. I wear a ring to remind me. It can be a piece of jewelry, an affirmation on a card in your pocket, a photo, a rubber band, a screen saver, anything.

I keep my afternoon ritual simple: I usually just go to a quiet place and say a prayer. My morning ritual, though, is more elaborate, even though it usually takes only fifteen minutes or less. I'll give it to you here — take it as one example among infinite possibilities, and modify it as you wish.

The power of ritual is that it keeps reminding us what we need to know, and wish to know. Ritual is a direct line to spirit, to God.

A MORNING RITUAL

My morning ritual has changed and evolved over the years, and keeps changing. When I was thirty, it was primarily an affirmation session, and didn't include prayer at all, except in the ways that affirmations in themselves are a form of prayer. I would list my goals and affirm that each one was manifesting, in an easy and relaxed manner, in a healthy and positive way. As we have seen, that process proved to be perfectly effective; I attained every goal in my ideal scene.

Over the years, I began to pray in these morning sessions, and more expansive results happened in my life even more quickly. Now, on a typical morning, here's my simple little ritual:

When I wake up, I first try to remember as much as possible from my dreams. If the dream is outstanding in some way, I'll get up and write it down. This is rare, though. Usually I just stay in bed, recall as much as I can of my dreams, and then deeply relax on my back.

I take a deep breath, and as I exhale, relax my body. I take another deep breath, and as I exhale, relax my mind. I take a third deep breath, and let go completely. I become aware of spirit, energy, presence within. Sometimes that's all I'll do, simply spend a few blessed moments being aware of the life force within. Other times I'll "run the energy," feel it moving through my body, and circulate it up one side and down the other. If something needs healing, I'll direct it into that part of my body.

Some mornings this leads to a longer guided meditation, a session of creative visualization that can go in innumerable directions — visualizing my new, revised, expanded ideal scene; praying for success for my next project or the solution to a puzzling challenge; asking to see the opportunity and benefit within what seems to be a problem; sending healing energy to a friend; even visualizing and praying for world peace and sweeping global changes.

Then I get out of bed, put on some old clothes, and head

out into my yard for a quiet little walk and prayer. As soon as I step outside, I stand motionless and let all thought go. This is relatively easy to do first thing in the morning. I have a moment of silence, where I simply observe the world around me. It is always fresh and beautiful, full of life. Only in silence can we truly appreciate the beauty of creation.

Then I start to walk and to pray. I always begin by thanking the Creator for the beautiful day, regardless of the weather. Then I usually give thanks for all the abundance that has been showered upon me, and I specifically mention several things I am thankful for.

This always puts me in an attitude of gratitude. It makes me aware that my list of what I'm grateful for is endless — I could spend the rest of my life recounting it, and never come to an end, because it includes every moment of my life and every molecule of creation, in its endless forms.

By this time, I usually reach my backyard, where I have a view of a mountain in the distance. I stop and let all thought go again, and take in the scene. It is different every morning, always changing. The mountain has become a wordless guiding force in my life.

Then I go back to conscious prayer, and I pray to do God's will, every moment. I ask, *What is Your will?* And then I take a deep breath, and let all thought go.

I always get an answer, almost immediately, in a still, small voice within, usually something like this:

"You know my will. It never changes: love, serve, and remember.
"Remember to love and serve, always.
"Remember the end of all wisdom is love, love, love.
"Remember the joy that comes in service.
"Remember who you are: a spiritual being in a physical body, a being of light."

At that point, I turn toward the sun, eyes closed, and feel its radiance in every cell of my body.

"Remember: To offer no resistance to life is to be in a state of grace, ease, and lightness."

God usually ends up quoting Eckhart Tolle to me! That phrase has become part of my prayer nearly every morning, and is something I often remember and reflect on through the day: Offer no resistance to life. This is the key to a life well lived, to a life of grace, ease, and lightness — and even to enlightenment, which isn't some distant goal, but the reality of our essential nature. It is who we really are: beings of light and spirit.

I usually end my morning ritual with the kind of affirmation session that was described in the beginning of this Course, though I often go in and shower or sometimes do some writing first. My mornings are completely flexible in this way. But at some time in the morning I usually take another five or ten minutes to stroll around and repeat the words that have had such an impact in my life — you'll notice this key is significantly different from the way it was stated earlier (Key 23) because of the final two words that have been added:

KEY 139

In an easy and relaxed manner,
in a healthy and positive way,
in its own perfect time,
for the highest good of all I pray . . .

Then I clearly express each one of my goals as affirmations.

I have five things on my list at the present. I'll give it to you as an example — find the wording that works for you. The words change, too, over time, and I often change the order, and focus on whichever one comes to mind.

· ·

1. *In an easy and relaxed manner... I am doing God's will, guided by Spirit every moment. This is enlightenment.*

2. *In an easy and relaxed manner... my company continues to grow, reaching $_____ in sales and $_____ in profits this year.*

3. *In an easy and relaxed manner... my books have a great impact in the world. I take a quantum leap in my writing success, selling over _____ copies of my books over the next two years.*

4. *In an easy and relaxed manner... my music is expressed beautifully, with grace, ease, and lightness. It takes a quantum leap in its success in the world and in personal satisfaction.*

5. *In an easy and relaxed manner... my marriage and family life and times alone are sources of great joy, grace, ease, and lightness.*

This is my complete list of goals at the moment I write this — it will have changed by the time you read this.

Each of them is preceded by the words *In an easy and relaxed manner, in a healthy and positive way, in its own perfect time, for the highest good of all I pray.*

At the end, I add the "cosmic insurance" clause: *This, or something better, is now manifesting, in totally satisfying and harmonious ways, for the highest good of all.*

And each day I become more and more aware of the phenomenal power of prayer.

> *Ask and it will be given you.*   KEY 140
> *Seek, and you will find.*
> *Knock, and it will be opened unto you.*
>
> — **Matthew 7:7**

DECLARATIONS

Declarations are a simple form of prayer. Once again, this key is found in the Bible, expressed fully, clearly, and simply:

KEY 141

And you shall decree a thing
and it will be established unto you,
and the light will shine upon your ways.

— Job 22:28

Decree, declaration: Using these kinds of tools you can become a king in his generativity, or a queen in her unlimited abundance, or a high priestess in her power, or a generous and compassionate millionaire — whatever you choose to imagine.

You issue a decree, and that decree is granted. This is the power of prayer.

So be it. So it is.

THE POWER OF MEDITATION

The effects of meditation are countless and endless. They are subtle and quiet, yet they can be extremely powerful, even life-changing in major ways.

Words are inadequate to describe the power of meditation. You can describe the taste of an orange to people who have never tasted it, but they will never know what you mean until they actually taste an orange. It is the same with meditation.

The teachers of meditation I have met rarely attempt to describe its effects or its power. They simply tell us to meditate, and discover it for ourselves.

Those who have gained at least some degree of mastery in meditation rarely tell you anything about their experiences in meditation — if they did, after all, we would probably sit there and expect something like it, and quite possibly miss our own unique experience.

A good teacher of meditation   KEY 142
just keeps pointing the way
for you to have your own experience:
Sit quietly, breathe.
Let all thought go.
Expect nothing. . . .
Carry this attitude into the rest of your life.

THE ESSENCE OF MEDITATION

Just sit. Even if just for a minute, even if just for one breath. Empty yourself, for a change. Instead of thinking all the time and doing things all the time, take a moment to relax, to let go and not think at all, to be quiet and receptive.

That is the essence of meditation.

Meditation isn't another activity you do. It's the opposite side of the polarity of activity: non-activity, stillness. Meditation is doing nothing.

Almost all of our time, except dreamless sleep, is spent in activity. It's good to take some time to experience the opposite side of the polarity. Sit quietly, do nothing. Be completely inactive for a while, and see what happens.

It's something every child does naturally — but then somewhere along the line most of us forget it and have to be reminded of it, repeatedly.

THE GREAT BENEFITS OF MEDITATION

Meditation has great benefits for us physically, emotionally, mentally, and spiritually. It reduces heart rate, blood pressure, and stress, and has proven to be healing in a great number of physical, mental, and emotional ways. It brings mental clarity to complex situations, and calmness to adverse situations.

Most important of all, it gives us wisdom and a peace that surpasses all understanding.

Obviously the only way to discover its effects is to try it. Simply sit and relax, without expectation, for any period of time, and soon you'll discover for yourself why meditation is important.

HOW TO MEDITATE

There are countless ways to meditate. Here are a range of them, for beginners and for those experienced in meditation as well. Explore any of them that feel right for you — the ones that feel comfortable, pleasant, easy, and relaxed. Find the simple way or ways that work for you.

BASIC, ESSENTIAL MEDITATION

Become aware of your breathing at this moment. Let your breath out slowly, and let all thought go. . . .

Do it again, with your next breath. Let all thought go. . . .

Find the space between thoughts, even if it's just momentary at first.

You have just meditated, even if just for two seconds. It's enough for a glimpse of your presence, your spirit.

Do it again. Do it often, throughout the day, if you can.

WATCHING YOUR THOUGHTS

We can add one more thing to it:

Become aware of your breathing at this moment. Let your breath out slowly, and let all thought go....

Do it again, with your next breath. Let all thought go.... Watch for the next thought that arises, with the attention of a cat watching a mouse hole.

When the next thought arises, let it go.... Find the space between your thoughts.

FINDING THE GAPS

Continue the practice above, with your eyes open or closed, for a minute, or however long you wish. When a thought arises, let it go and return to your breath.

If you continue to do this simple practice, you'll find longer and longer gaps between your thoughts. Within that gap is silence, stillness, awareness, light.

Relax into the light.

This light is what we really are. We are not just our physical bodies — we are light.

COUNTING BREATHS

Here is a traditional Zen meditation, excellent for beginners and even for those who have meditated for years.

Sit quietly, close your eyes. As you breathe out, count *one.* Let go of all thought as you breathe in, and as you breathe out again, count *two*. Count to ten this way, finding as much stillness as you can as you inhale. After ten breaths, start counting over again with *one*.

If you are a beginner, you probably won't get past counting to three or four before you will wander off into some labyrinth of thought. Just let the thought go and start over from one. In a short time you'll find you can go longer and longer before you wander off into thought. Counting breaths gives you a simple, clear way to see your progress.

FINDING STILLNESS WITHIN

Sit comfortably. Close your eyes. Take a deep breath, and relax your body as you exhale. Take another deep breath, and relax your whole body/mind as you exhale. Take another breath, and let all thought go. With every succeeding breath, just keep letting go.

You soon find the space between your thoughts, and as you keep sitting you're able to remain in that space for longer and longer periods.

At some point, you'll discover a deep quiet stillness within, a place Zen teachers call *samadhi*. It is not sleep, though it is as rejuvenating as sleep; you are highly aware, completely conscious, and yet deeply relaxed.

Keep sitting and relax...into *samadhi*.

Call that deep stillness what you will. It is beyond thought, and therefore beyond words. Yet we want to try to describe everything in our experience, so here are a few possibilities, among many:

Life	Life energy
Presence	The Tao
Being	Great Spirit
Spirit	Ultimate reality
God	The quantum field
Creator	Light body
The Source	*Samadhi*
Christ consciousness	Spiritual nature
Buddha nature	The Force
Higher power	The Mother Wave

Take your pick. Or come up with something else. Or don't name it anything at all.

When thoughts arise, just observe: Your mind has become active again. Relax more deeply as you slowly breathe out, and let go of the thought, let go of all activity.

Take some time to be still, to do nothing. Keep sitting, expecting nothing — and someday you'll discover an ocean of serenity within. You'll discover a peace that arises within, naturally, easily, effortlessly, a vibrant presence that is abiding and eternal.

Through meditation, we discover our spirit, the glorious part of us that lives forever.

FLOODING YOUR BODY WITH CONSCIOUSNESS

When you are unoccupied for a few minutes, and especially last thing at night before falling asleep and first thing in the morning before getting up, "flood" your body with consciousness.

Close your eyes. Lie flat on your back. Choose different parts of your body to focus your attention on, briefly at first: hands, feet, arms, legs, abdomen, chest, head, and so on. Feel the life energy inside those parts as intensely as you can. Stay with each part for fifteen seconds or so.

Then let your attention run through the body like a wave a few times, from feet to head and back again. This need only take a minute or so. After that, feel the inner body in its totality, as a single field of energy. Hold that feeling for a few minutes.

Be intensely present during that time, present in every cell of your body.*

GOING INTO THE REALM OF PURE BEING

Take at least ten or fifteen minutes for this meditation. Find a place where there are no external distractions such as telephones or people who are likely to interrupt you. Sit on a chair, but don't lean back. Keep the spine erect; it helps you stay alert. Or choose your own favorite position for meditation. Lying flat on your back is fine as well.

Relax your body. Close your eyes. Take a few deep breaths. Feel yourself breathing into the lower abdomen, as it were. Observe how it expands and contracts with each in and out breath.

Then become aware of the entire inner energy field of your body. Don't think about it — feel it. By

---

* This meditation and the one that follows are reprinted, with permission, from *The Power of Now* by Eckhart Tolle. Both are also in *Practicing the Power of Now.*

doing this, you reclaim consciousness from the mind. If you find it helpful, repeat the previous meditation, and flood your body with life energy.

When you can feel the inner body clearly as a single field of energy, let go, if possible, of any visual image and focus exclusively on the feeling. If you can, also drop any mental image you may still have of the physical body. All that is left then is an all-encompassing sense of presence, of "beingness," and the inner body is felt to be without a boundary.

Then take your attention even more deeply into that feeling. Become one with it. Merge with the energy field, so that there is no longer a perceived duality of the observer and the observed, of you and your body. The distinction between inner and outer also dissolves now, so there is no inner body anymore. By going deeply into the body, you have transcended the body.

Stay in this realm of pure Being for as long as feels comfortable.

Then become aware again of the physical body, your breathing and physical senses, and open your eyes. Look at your surroundings for a few minutes in a meditative way — that is, without labeling things mentally — and continue to feel the inner body as you do so.

THROUGHOUT THE DAY

Eckhart Tolle is one of the greatest teachers of meditation I have ever met. The two meditations above are from his work. Another great teacher I had was Katsuki Sekida, who taught at the Honolulu and Maui Zendos in the 1960s, and at the London Zen Society from 1970 to 1972, and wrote two great books, *Zen Training* and *Two Zen Classics*.

In *Zen Training,* he describes in great detail how, after sitting in meditation for a while, we naturally enter into a state of *absolute samadhi,* where we are completely conscious, silent, and aware.

Then, as we get up and go into the activity of our day, we can train ourselves to be in a state of what he describes as *positive samadhi,* where there is no extraneous thought in our mind as we are focused on the object of our attention, whatever it may be.

> Throughout the day, take a moment to let go of all thought as often as you can. It can be as simple and as short as a single exhalation: Let your thought go as you let your breath go.
>
> Look outside first thing in the morning, take a deep breath, and let all thought go as you exhale.
>
> During your affirmation or prayer session in the morning, stepping into the shower, sitting down with a cup of coffee or tea, turning on your computer, getting into your car — take a deep breath, and let all thought go as you exhale.
>
> As you finish a phone call or a small task, take a deep breath, and let all thought go before you go onto something else.
>
> Remind yourself throughout the day to let go of thought as much as possible. Find moments, even if very brief, to sit in silence.

POSITIVE SAMADHI

When you walk up a stairs, simply walk, without extraneous thought. Whatever you are doing, simply focus on that, without letting your mind wander into streams of thoughts about other things.

ATTAINING ENLIGHTENMENT ON THE FREEWAY

Suzuki Roshi, founder of the San Francisco Zen Center, was another great teacher of meditation. He and Katsuki Sekida were very much alike in many ways; both had an ocean of serenity surrounding them, regardless of external circumstances, and both found a great deal of humor in life.

One time Suzuki Roshi mentioned Zen *koans,* the little phrases and stories some students of Zen meditate on. Then he smiled and said this:

> *Here's a* **koan** *for Westerners:*   KEY 143
> *How do I attain enlightenment driving on the freeway?*

I have asked myself that question many times over many years while driving on the freeway, or on any kind of road.

Over the years I've gotten many, many different answers. Some can be expressed in words; most can't. Often all thought simply falls away. I drive with complete awareness of the vehicle and the road, but without a thought in my mind.

Next time you're driving, ask yourself that question. See what happens.

FEEL THE LOVE IN YOUR HEART

Sit quietly, relax, and become aware of your heart.

Feel its vibrant presence. Feel it fill with radiant healing energy. Feel it radiate its warmth. That warmth is love.

Feel the love in your heart. Feel that love expand to include the whole Earth, and then even all of creation. You are in the heart of God.

SEE THE PRESENCE

Sit quietly, relax. Close your eyes and become aware of the vibrant light energy that is centered between your eyes. This is your "third eye," the eye of inner vision.

What do you see with your eyes closed? What do you see with your inner vision?

If what you see is formless, you are seeing God in its ultimate formless state.

If you see something with form, you are seeing a form of God.

A yoga teacher in India put it so simply in the film *Phantom India* directed by Louis Malle:

KEY 144   *Close your eyes, and see God.*

Feel yourself in the presence of the One who created it all. Sit quietly in the still radiance.

Ask that presence, if you wish, for guidance, answers, support. It is omnipresent, all knowing, and all powerful.

LOOK WITHIN

Sit quietly, close your eyes, relax. Become aware of the radiant energy, the presence, within you.

Within your inner world is endless, everlasting energy and information, directly connected to the source of all creation, an integral part of the entire quantum field of the universe.

To access that energy, simply look within, ask your question or ask for guidance, and wait for an answer. It will come, sooner or later.

Return to your center within. Feel its presence. Feel the energy in your body. Keep letting thought go as it arises. Keep returning to your center. You are filled with light within. Feel its peace and power.

THE VAST OCEAN OF STILLNESS WITHIN

Sit quietly and comfortably. Close your eyes. Breathe slowly and deeply for a while. . . . Relax. . . . Let yourself go. . . .

Become aware of your breathing, and let it go deeper and deeper within. Let your breath fall deep within you. Let your exhalations become longer and longer. Breathe deeply, and let go, into stillness. . . .

Imagine, if you want to, a vast ocean of stillness within. Become one with the vast silent ocean within.

There is a Zen *koan* that says, *Pick up the silent rock from the depths of the sea and, without getting your sleeves wet, bring it up to me.*

MEDITATION IN MOTION

As you walk, imagine a vast ocean within you. It radiates out of the depth of your belly. It is silent, still, and endlessly deep.

As you move, imagine the ocean encompassing all you see, and even all there is.

We are one in a vast ocean of a single quantum field, filled with energy and information. We become receptive to it when we quiet our mind.

I once read a *koan* on a bathroom wall in Northern California:

In motion be like water, in stillness like a mirror.

GIVING UP RESISTANCE

We've seen this phrase before, from *The Power of Now* by Eckhart Tolle. It's worth meditating on until we understand it so deeply it affects every moment of our lives:

As you sit quietly and as you go about your day, reflect on this phrase:

KEY 105

*To offer no resistance to life
is to be in a state of grace, ease, and lightness.*

Throughout the day, when you find yourself resisting something — whether it's a big thing, like a major loss in your life, or a small thing, like the cat peeing on the carpet — bring those words back into your mind, and let go of your resistance.

Resist nothing.

THE JOY OF BEING

After you've pondered that great key for a while, move on to this one from *The Power of Now:*

The happiness that is derived from some secondary source KEY 106
is never very deep.
It is only a pale reflection of the joy of Being,
the vibrant peace that you find within
as you enter a state of nonresistance.

Nothing out there in the world — no other person, great wealth, prestige, or anything else — can bring us lasting happiness. It can only be found within.

CREATIVE VISUALIZATION

All the forms of meditation above involve letting thought go as it arises. There are forms of meditation, however, that use focused thought: one is creative visualization, another is reflecting on specific phrases. We've already done both of these types of meditation many times in this Course.

When we use creative visualization, we relax deeply and then focus on what we want to create in our life. When we visualize our ideal scene, we are doing this meditation: We're imagining, envisioning, what we want in life. The more we do it, the greater detail we bring to our imagined reality — and the sooner we receive clear instructions on how to create that reality.

Take a deep breath, and relax deeply as you exhale. Close your eyes, and take a few more deep, relaxing breaths. Imagine your life, in vivid detail, five years in the future. Imagine yourself enjoying new levels of success, health, and fulfillment.

Visualize sending healing energy to a friend who needs it; visualize their disease dissolving into light; see them as strong and healthy again.

This kind of visualization and prayer where you send healing energy to others has been proven to be effective in scientific double-blind studies of the effects of prayer in healing. And it has proven to be effective in the lives of countless people who regularly practice this type of meditation, myself included.[*]

REFLECTING ON A PHRASE

We've been doing this type of active meditation almost constantly throughout this Course: Take a specific phrase and repeat it, reflecting on the words.

> Pick any one of the keys in this Course that appeals to you and repeat it until you understand it, and its meaning takes root in your subconscious.

> Once that happens, surprising change occurs in your life, automatically, easily and effortlessly.

CREATING AN INNER ALTAR

Here's one you can adapt endlessly to your own wishes, desires, and understanding. You simply create your own imaginary altar, and put whatever images on it you choose.

> Close your eyes, take a long, slow breath, and relax. Take another breath, and relax more and more deeply as you exhale.

---

* For much more on these forms of meditation, see *Creative Visualization* and other works of Shakti Gawain; also see *The Art of True Healing* by Israel Regardie.

Imagine before you an image of God — as you choose to see God in this moment — on an inner altar of some kind. Sit quietly, bathing in the radiance of God as you see God.

If you wish, imagine that altar expanding to include other images of the sacred that occur to you. Imagine many images of all that is sacred, if you wish. Sit quietly in the radiance of these images.

Whatever images come to mind are images of God — it's all God. If there are no images, then you are seeing the ultimate body of God: formlessness.

Bathe in the silent light of God's radiance. You are sitting in the heart of God.

FORM AND FORMLESSNESS

Sit quietly, and observe the world within. When forms arise, remember: It is all a part of God. It too is formless, in its essence. All form is essentially empty.

Reflect on these words from a famous Buddhist sutra that some students of Zen chant:

> *Form is emptiness.*　　　　　　　KEY 145
> *Emptiness is form.*

CARING AND NOT CARING

The poet T. S. Eliot wrote these words in his poem *Ash Wednesday*. In a play I was in years ago, we turned these words into a little song or mantra we chanted over and over, and it proved to be a good meditation practice:

Teach us to care, and not to care.
Teach us to sit still.

LEARN TO BE QUIET

There are keys everywhere. We can find guidance for a life well lived all over the place, sometimes in the most unexpected places. The famous writer Franz Kafka came up with these striking and powerful words:

You need not leave your room.
Remain sitting at your table and listen.
You need not even listen, simply wait.
You need not even wait, just learn to be quiet
and still and solitary.

The world will freely offer itself to you
to be unmasked. It has no choice;
it will roll in ecstasy at your feet.

— Franz Kafka

LET THERE BE PEACE

Over the years I have attended many services in many different kinds of churches. All of them have some forms of prayer, and most of them encourage some kind of meditation.

In Unity Churches, they have a song they sing at every service that contains a beautiful phrase to meditate on. Bring these words to mind as often as possible — the more of us do it, the sooner we can transform the world.

Let there be peace on earth,
And let it begin with me.

THE POWER OF RELAXATION

There are great benefits to relaxation, whether in brief moments throughout the day or in longer periods when we rest at home or take vacations. It's certainly worthwhile to luxuriate in the healing power of relaxation.

PRESCRIPTION FOR A TYPE-A CULTURE

We can put it this way for all those entrenched in our workaholic culture: When we relax, whether for even just brief moments or for longer periods, *the important work is still getting done.* In fact, it's often the best way, the most efficient way, to do the work, in the long run.

Throughout the day, especially in the midst of what seems to be a problem or stressful situation, learn to relax for a moment, even for just one breath. Take a deep, healing breath and slowly let it go, and let go of all thought along with your breath.

That's it — just one breath. Two or three breaths is even better. Just let go of your thoughts for a moment. When you start thinking again, you just might have a clearer perspective on the problem; it might be much simpler to find the solution than you thought it was. You've done an important bit of work in that moment of relaxation.

We all know the value of sleeping on something. So often something that seems problematic in the afternoon is much less complicated, much clearer in the morning. The same thing can happen in a breath, or in two or three breaths, for in that brief time a creative new solution has some room to emerge.

This is an excellent little habit to develop:

Take a deep breath and relax.
Let all thought go for the moment.
Do this several times throughout the day.

As Eckhart Tolle puts it in *The Power of Now,* "When you are full of problems there is no room for anything new to enter, no room for a solution. So whenever you can, make some room, create some space...."

BRIEF RELAXING MOMENTS THROUGHOUT THE DAY

The best thing you can do in the midst of your activity is to relax for a moment, and let go of everything, even all thought.

Just a single deep breath lowers blood pressure and relieves stress. Just letting your thoughts go for a brief moment can open you up to a clearer perspective. Two or three deep breaths is even better, a quiet minute or two is better yet.

Find times throughout your day when you can relax. When you have a bathroom break, you can turn it into a refreshing moment of quiet meditation.

Sometimes during the day I put on a tape or go to my website and close my eyes and listen to a few minutes of my stress reduction tape or music. (I love to listen to my own music, I must admit.) And Sanaya Roman and Duane Packer have a website I often visit (www.orindaben.com) that has a whole series of short two- or three-minute meditations you can choose from that are tremendously relaxing.

Just as research has shown even a minute or two of vigorous exercise can make a big difference in your energy level, even a minute of relaxation can have a calming effect that lasts for hours.

LONGER PERIODS OF RESTING

Any amount of resting is rejuvenating, whether it's for a minute or an hour or anywhere in between. I always encourage people to take more naps — there are times during the day when our bodies want to relax, and we often ignore those signals.

Relax more and you'll stay healthier. It's much better in the long run to relax when you feel like it than to take more stimulants and power through it. You don't work very well anyway when you're tired; you're slow and inefficient. It is far better to rest, and then come back when you're physically and emotionally up for it.

We used to have a tradition of Sunday as a day of rest, but somehow many of us have lost that tradition. Let's bring it back. After all:

> *We all need a day of rest.*   KEY 150
> *Even God needed a day of rest.*

Sunday is a day of rest, prayer, and family for me. And Monday is my day alone, to rest or do whatever I feel like in the moment. I always end Monday with a sauna or hot tub, and then put my son to bed.

There have been days when I've gotten up, had a strong cup of coffee, and then gone back to bed. My family thinks this behavior is funny. To me it's the most natural thing in the world, and I encourage everyone to nap as much as possible. We can learn a lot from our cats and dogs. A catnap during the day is highly refreshing.

I keep my mornings during the week to myself, for sleeping, meditating, writing, goofing off, doing whatever I feel like doing in the moment.

I don't get to the office until Tuesday afternoon, but by

then I am ready to work, energized and enthused, and plow through sixty e-mails and twenty phone messages and a stack of mail. Because I'm fully rested, I work efficiently and effectively. Sometimes I'll work for over ten hours, until midnight, though I always leave as soon as I feel like relaxing.

VACATIONS

We all need vacations! Our souls need vacations.

We have seen that many of the processes we use in this Course, from the first step on, involve long-range planning. First we set our long-term goals and make our long-term plans, then we break them down into the next obvious steps to take in the short-term. It is essential to make those long-term plans and to keep them in mind.

Vacations give our hearts and minds time to reflect on the long-range things that are so vital to us. They can put our lives into clearer perspective; sometimes they can lead to bold decisions and sweeping changes.

Once we have a plan clearly in mind, important work on that plan continues to be done whether we're working away on it or sitting on a warm beach — and sometimes we make quantum leaps during a vacation that wouldn't have occurred to us if we were working as usual.

KEY 151

Take a vacation!
It's good for business, pleasure, and health.

THE JOY OF BEING A SEMI-HERMIT

From the very first ideal scene I imagined at age thirty, an important part of it all was living a life of ease and relaxation — a slower-paced life, with lots of time for my family and for myself as well. What good is having a beautiful home if you're working constantly and don't have time to enjoy it?

Over the years, the personal part of my ideal became even clearer to me, and I realized I wanted to be on a retreat about half the time. To me, it's a perfect balance: half the time retreating quietly, half the time in action.

This goal has come true for me — I have now realized my dream of becoming a half-time hermit. I have plenty of time alone, plenty of time for meditation, relaxation, sleep, reading, goofing off.

These rules have evolved for my retreats: I am alone. I don't go anywhere. I have no plans. I don't get on the Internet or do e-mail (I keep my Internet access at the office, and don't even have it at home). I meditate sometime during the day, and sleep whenever I want to. I write, and wander around the yard. I take a sauna or hot tub, usually, in the evening.

After even just a day or two of retreat, I'm always rested, energized, and ready to go wherever I want or need to go — in an easy and relaxed manner, in a healthy and positive way.

A CALL TO INACTION

I've said it before: This is a call to inaction as well as a call to action.

For thousands of years in China, the leading philosophers and teachers have clearly understood the great polarities that are always at work in our lives and our world. I've mentioned this before, but it bears reflecting on again as we close this chapter.

Each polarity contains the seed of the other. Each *defines* the other: Without dark, there is no light. The universe is an endless dance of light and dark, creation and destruction, activity and stillness — *yang* and *yin.*

There is a great polarity of action and stillness at work in the universe. In our culture, most of us have gotten very good at focusing on the active part of the polarity, but ignore the other part: inaction, rest, relaxation, meditation, receptivity, stillness.

Within this side of the polarity we find tremendous rejuvenation, light, and meaning in our lives.

KEY 152

Be still,
and you will find tremendous rejuvenation,
understanding, and light.

Think about these words, then let those thoughts take you beyond all thought, into a quiet, calm stillness. It is one of the very best things you can do for your physical, mental, and emotional health.

Add any notes or quotes from this lesson that you particularly want to remember into your folder. Review it often.

SUMMARY

- We are spiritual beings as well as physical beings. We know this at birth, we know it at death, but sometimes we forget in between.
- When we witness someone dying, we touch the sacred; if we've had a near-death experience ourselves, we know we have a spirit that lives forever. Call it what you will; it is beyond any label we can give it.
- We're vastly complex and multifaceted, with four different levels of being: physical, emotional, mental, and spiritual. It's good to reflect on this, because

there are truly powerful keys to be discovered here —
life-altering keys, tools for transformation.

- We are all psychic, to some degree. We just need to
tune in to our feelings for a wealth of intuitive knowledge and psychic information.

- As the poet John Milton wrote, "The mind is its own
place, and can create a heaven of hell, a hell of
heaven." The mind is a wonderful tool, a great servant, but not a good master. The mind needs to be
guided by the spirit.

- Prayer, in whatever form you choose, gives you access
to the creative forces of the universe. This is the
power of prayer. When you pray you connect with
spirit, and set in motion the mysterious forces that
answer your prayer.

- It is a very good practice to start the day with a ritual
of some kind that acknowledges and remembers your
spirit. It's good to have an afternoon or evening ritual
as well. And it's very good to have something that reminds you of spirit throughout the day.

- The effects of meditation are endless. They are subtle
and quiet, yet they can be extremely powerful, even
life-changing in major ways. Meditation has great
benefits for us physically, emotionally, and mentally.

- Simply sit and relax, without expectation, for any period of time, and you'll discover for yourself why
meditation is important.

- There are great benefits to relaxation as well, whether
in brief moments throughout the day or in longer periods of rest at home or on vacation.

- Here's a good assignment: Find some moments to
regularly breathe deeply and relax, even if just for one

or two breaths, throughout the day. Relax more and you'll stay healthier. Make Sunday or some day a day of rest. Even God needed a day of rest.

- We all need vacations! Our souls need vacations. Important soul work gets done on vacation. Vacations are good for business, pleasure, and health. Take your own form of retreats, as well, as often as you need.
- This Course is a call to inaction as well as a call to action: *Go forth and do nothing* — at least for a while.
- Be still, and you will find tremendous rejuvenation — as well as understanding and light.

We are not physical beings

who may have a spiritual experience;

We are spiritual beings

having a physical experience.

— Pierre Teilhard de Chardin

. . . .

Do What You Love to Do, and Success Will Follow; You Can Transform Your Life and Your World by Doing What You Love to Do

DISCOVER WHAT YOU LOVE TO DO

Some of the material in this final lesson is similar to what we've discussed in Lesson 3, but with a different emphasis. In Lesson 3, we focused on the powerful words *vocation* and *purpose*. Here we'll simplify, and put this great key in these words: *Find what you truly love to do, and do it.*

You already know what you really love to do, though you may have to do a bit of soul searching to recollect it. It's in your heart, it's in your soul. It's in your fantasies.

What do you really enjoy doing in your spare time?

What kind of work has fascinated you?

What things *excite* you? Is there something that gets you as excited as a puppy or a baby can be?

If you could do anything, what would it be?

If, even after answering these questions, you're still not sure what your passion is, you may have to go on some kind of quest. (We covered this earlier, in Lesson 3.) Or this simple little exercise (also mentioned in the same lesson) might do it for you:

Imagine you just won the lottery.
Lack of money is no longer a factor at all.
What will you do?

Think it through. A lot of people will say, "I'd go relax on a beach," or "I'd travel around the world."

Stay with it. Ask yourself: *And then what?*

After relaxing and traveling for a while, what do you want to do?

Can you imagine the next five years of your life? Can you imagine the entire scope of a possible lifetime stretched out before you?

What kind of person do you want to be? What do you want to have accomplished at the end of it all? What do you want to be remembered for?

Within the answers to these questions are the things you love to do.

THE ANSWERS ARE WITHIN YOU

No one else can tell you what you love to do. The answer is in your dreams and fantasies — what do you sometimes imagine yourself doing? The answer is in your ideal scene. The answer is even in the people you envy — do you find yourself jealous of someone's success? If you do, it's usually because they're doing what you would like to be doing. Otherwise, why would you be jealous of them?

Remember what Ralph Waldo Emerson said: You would not have a deep, driving desire or recurring fantasy if you didn't also have the capability of fulfilling it.

Remember what Deepak Chopra said: Within every desire is the seed and mechanics for its fulfillment.

> *Do what you love to do.*   KEY 155
> *Keep doing it.*
> *Make it an intention that it will*
> *support you abundantly.*
> *Look for a way to do it*
> *and you will be led to it, step by step.*

Can it really be this simple? Yes, it can — and, oddly enough, the reason it remains so elusive for most people seems to be because of its simplicity. It takes very few words to speak the truth — and here's the simple truth, something you've heard many times before:

Ask and you will receive; seek and you will find.

CAN THIS REALLY WORK FOR YOU?

If you understand this simple key and apply it in your life, you'll find it working wonders: *Keep thinking about your dreams — what you think about expands.* The next step to take becomes clear to you, and you move, easily and effortlessly, toward realization of your goal, your dream.

It's obvious when we see it — and when we do what we love to do, we find life works out perfectly, in extraordinary ways we couldn't even have imagined before. There are a great many people who have built successful careers doing whatever it is you love to do. Look at the ones who are successful, and reflect on the unique way or ways you too can be successful.

Take the first step you can toward doing what you love to do. That step will lead you to the next step. Opportunities will appear. You will find support in new and unexpected ways. You are on your way.

THE ATTITUDE THAT BRINGS SUCCESS

Having the right attitude will bring you success: Acknowledge — and celebrate! — that you have something unique to offer the world. There is no one like you. You have unique abilities, talents, and gifts.

Keep remembering that many others have been successful doing whatever it is you want to do, and applaud them and learn from them, taking what works for you. They are your mentors, and they can show you a great number of very different ways to be successful doing what you love to do.

Through it all, keep more attention on the full half of the glass than the empty half. Remember: What you think about expands.

WHY AREN'T MORE PEOPLE SUCCESSFUL?

Why don't more people succeed in doing what they love to do? Isn't it because, underneath it all, it's so hard to succeed? Aren't the odds really against us? There's so much competition out there, after all, and so many others who are so good at what they're doing.

The simple reason why more people aren't more successful is that, because of the conditioning most of us got in our education, home lives, and culture in general, most of us picked up a large bundle of limiting beliefs, and we habitually see the half-empty part of the glass. Most of us are so acutely aware of our shortcomings and of the problems and difficulties inherent in any expansive goal that we don't even dare to dream, much less take some steps toward fulfilling our dreams.

Most of us fear failure, and most of us don't even try. Instead of fearing failure, we should celebrate it! We have an invaluable skill when we can learn how to fail with grace,

ease, and lightness. Everyone who has succeeded has had failures along the way. They are an essential part of our education.

Those that try and keep trying usually have some failures,
but they inevitably succeed. We've all heard this so often it
feels like a cliché: *If at first you don't succeed, try and try again.*

Or, as the great comic actor Burt Lahr (who played the
Cowardly Lion in *The Wizard of Oz*) put it:

> *Stay on the merry-go-round long enough,*   KEY 156
> *and you're bound to get the brass ring.*

It is inevitable, if you keep trying. You'll probably fail at
first, but then you'll get the hang of it and eventually get that
brass ring or Olympic gold or royalty check or whatever it
may be that acknowledges you have attained the dream you
have affirmed and intended in your heart.

Keep affirming your dreams will manifest, in an easy and
relaxed manner, for the highest good of all.

WHAT ABOUT SERVICE?

As soon as we have a dream, the steps we take toward it
inevitably involve work and service of some kind. But if we're
really doing what we love, work becomes rewarding and enjoyable — and service becomes the greatest joy of all, because
we are serving ourselves as well as all humanity and God.

Earlier (in Lesson 9) we saw the great insight into service
that the great Indian poet Rabindranath Tagore had — it is
worth repeating and remembering:

> *I slept and dreamt that life was joy,*   KEY 116
> *I awoke and found that life was service.*
> *I acted, and behold! Service became joy.*
>
> — **Rabindranath Tagore**

THE ULTIMATE PURPOSE

Occasionally it's good to sit down and take the longest perspective possible. We can do this by asking a few good questions:

What is our purpose, ultimately? Were we born to fulfill something? To grow in a certain way?

You can only find the answers in your own words, of course. If not now, maybe they'll come when you overhear someone's casual remark, or see a striking ad somewhere, or in a dream. This is the answer I get, tailored to my life and way of looking at the world:

KEY 157

> *Our purpose is to evolve into something greater,*
> *to transform our lives and our world for the better.*

Your answer may be quite different. But I'm sure in some way it contains expansion, growth, fulfillment.

This Course contains not only the keys for all the monetary success we wish for, but for fulfillment of our ultimate purpose as well. And that's what is truly important in life, isn't it? It is far beyond money, beyond wealth. Money is only a tool to use to create something far more important than the tool itself.

The important thing is to live a life we can look back on with satisfaction and affection and love, and even with grace, ease, and lightness.

A DREAM

I had a dream, as I was completing the first draft of this manuscript. A year later, it still often comes to mind:

There are thousands of us, all working together in a smooth, easy partnership, building a vast new structure. The foundations have already been laid; we are beginning to build the walls that reached upward.

The building is going quickly, with ease and lightness, and as we build we listen to the words of the greatest visionaries of all times. It's almost as if they're being broadcast in some way, and we're hearing them together. Yet it is also very quiet, and it seems as if the words of the prophets are a whisper within us.

We are being guided by the greatest lights of our time: Jesus, Buddha, Mohammed, the great authors of the Vedas, the Torah, the Bible, indigenous peoples the world over, and the modern teachers, Thoreau, Gandhi, Martin Luther King, Eckhart Tolle, Riane Eisler, Shakti Gawain, the list goes on and on....

We are creating a new world, finding new ways to live in harmony with each other — a world where we work in partnership, with love and compassion for each other, and for the earth itself.

As we learn what all the great teachers of the perennial philosophy have to tell us, we can create a world where hunger and poverty are myths from the past, and we can discover better ways to take care of each other.

We can finish building the structure — it is a work in progress — necessary to fulfill Buckminster Fuller's goal of a world in which everyone on Earth improves their standard of living, and we all have an ever-better quality of life as we move up the pyramid of evolution.

It's time to be guided by a vision and spirit that brings us all together in partnership. After all, we're stuck with each other — we're one big global dysfunctional family, and we've got to learn to live together without killing each other, or abusing each other in any way. Only by having respect for each other and by living and working in partnership can we have a life of peace and plenty, which is what we all want.

It's happening now: As soon as we see it, as soon as we begin to imagine this new world, it begins to happen in our lives. Then it spreads out to the world.

It is happening already, and it will happen more and more extensively as more people have the dream and see the vision — the vision of a great number of us working in partnership to make our lives far more satisfying and to make the world a far better place. This is a key worth repeating:

KEY 158   *It is happening already, more and more extensively as more people have the dream or see the vision — the vision of a great number of us working in partnership to make our lives far more satisfying and the world a far better place.*

The vision, the collective thought, is reaching critical mass, and once that happens our lives and our world will change very quickly. We are on the verge of a global evolutionary leap — for growth and evolution is not a slow, steady process, it goes by leaps and bounds instead.

It might be ten years — it might be fifty or a hundred — before the global wake-up call that began in the last half of the twentieth century has global impact. Who knows how long it will take? It is happening in its own perfect time, for the highest good of all.

IT ALL BEGINS WITH A DREAM

It all begins with a dream, and continues as the dream continues. Find the courage that is somewhere within you to dream the greatest dreams you can, and then take whatever steps you can to move toward them. What could be more fulfilling?

First dream, then imagine possibilities and plans,   KEY 159
then move forward on your plans —
and you'll soon create the life of your dreams.

SUMMARY

- Discover what you love to do. You already know what it is, though you may have to do a bit of soul searching to recollect it. If you could do anything, what would it be? If you won the lottery, what would you do?
- Do what you love to do. Keep doing it. Make it an intention that it will support you abundantly. Look for a way to do it and you will be led to it, step by step.
- The reason most of these keys remain mysterious is not that we haven't heard them, but because they are so simple. Here's the simple truth: *Ask and you will receive; seek and you will find.*
- As soon as you affirm a goal, you are creating a thought, and your thoughts have powerful effects within you and in your world.
- Keep remembering your dreams. Acknowledge — and celebrate! — that you have something unique to offer the world. You have unique abilities, talents, and gifts.

- Keep doing what you love to do. When you do what you love, you find life works out perfectly, in extraordinary ways you can't even imagine at first.

- Most of us fear failure, but let's celebrate it instead! We can learn how to fail with grace, ease, and lightness. Everyone who has succeeded has had failures along the way. They are an essential part of our education.

- Those that try and keep trying usually have some failures, but they inevitably succeed. We've all heard this before! *If at first you don't succeed, try and try again.*

- It is inevitable: If you keep trying, you'll probably fail at first, but eventually you'll get the brass ring or whatever it may be that acknowledges you have attained the dream you have affirmed and intended in your heart.

- Our ultimate purpose is to evolve into something greater, to transform our lives and our world for the better.

- The important thing is to live a life we can look back on with affection and satisfaction and love, and even with grace, ease, and lightness.

- More and more of us are beginning to see how we can work in partnership. A vision of a world working in partnership is beginning to emerge in the collective thought. As soon as it reaches critical mass, we will quickly make a global evolutionary leap. Prepare yourself for some startling and truly marvelous results.

LIVING THE LIFE OF YOUR DREAMS – STEPS TO WEALTH AND FULFILLMENT

(1) Imagine your ideal scene; list and affirm your goals.

(2) Write your plan as a simple, clear visualization.

(3) Discover your vocation and purpose.

(4) See the full half of the glass, the benefits in adversity, and keep picturing success.

(5) Live and work in partnership with all.

(6) Avoid management by crisis with clear goals and transparency.

(7) Love change and learn to dance.

(8) Discover your core beliefs, and learn how to change them.

(9) Grow at your own pace, with an architecture of abundance.

(10) Give abundantly and reap the rewards: Put "The Ten Percent Solution" to work in your life.

(11) Become more aware of the spiritual side of life, the power of prayer, meditation, and relaxation.

(12) Do what you love to do, and success will follow. You can transform your life and your world by doing what you love to do.

It is happening already,

as more people have the dream

and see the vision —

the vision of a great number of us

working in partnership

to make our lives far more satisfying

and the world a far better place.

How the Process Works

At the core of this Course is a simple process. I have seen repeatedly — in my own life and in many others — that it works, but I have yet to fully understand how. Perhaps at its core it will always remain a mystery, for we are dealing with the forces of creation — the same forces that created our bodies, our minds, our emotional lives, our spirit, our world, the galaxies, the universe.

But in at least one way the process is clear to me:

When you imagine your ideal scene, when you clearly state and affirm a goal, you are in effect asking your subconscious mind to show you the next step toward that ideal scene and goal.

With the power of your thoughts and words, you are able to access something deep within you, deep within the core of the process of creation, and ask for its guidance and assistance. You can express this process in many different ways, with many different words, depending on your background and preferences:

You can say you are conditioning your subconscious, or programming your bio-computer, or planting seeds of thought in your creative mind, asking your intuition for guidance, connecting to the source of all creation, asking in prayer, petitioning to a higher power, declaring to the creative forces of the universe, summoning your guiding spirits, aligning yourself with the quantum field, opening yourself up to the field of all possibilities. You can say you are tuning into the force that guides the galaxies, and using it to guide you.

Put it any way you want, but once you start to use these tools, you will be guided, every step of the way — by intuition, by spirit, by your subconscious mind, by God, by the Tao, call it what you will.

Nearly every morning I take a stroll and say a little prayer. That prayer is my petition to the universe. Nearly every morning — or sometime throughout the day — I affirm, *In an easy and relaxed manner, in a healthy and positive way, in its own perfect time, for the highest good of all I pray —* and then I state my goals.

The first time I say a new goal, I know it's a good goal for me if I feel a bit of excitement, a thrill of new possibility. If it's a challenging, expansive goal, doubts and fears come up, but the words *in an easy and relaxed manner, in a healthy and positive way, in its own perfect time, for the highest good of all* have a way of diminishing those doubts and fears, and eventually even eliminating most of them.

After a few weeks or a few months of affirming the goal, an inner shift happens, easily and effortlessly, and what was a distant dream has now somehow become a very good possibility. It has become realizable, in an easy and relaxed manner, and the next steps to take are obvious. Over time, what had been a fantasy becomes an intention. And my intuition, or the universe, call it what you will, starts sending me messages about my goal. It may be as general as suggesting it's time to write a brief plan — and then I will quickly be shown the plan — or it may be as specific as nudging me to contact a certain person with a question or suggestion. It may be some other person coming in out of the blue who wants to help me in some way with my plan.

The goal has obviously been planted in my subconscious mind, and forces that are beyond my normal waking consciousness are at work on it. Then the fun begins.

CREATING OPPORTUNITIES

At some point in this process — usually after just two or three weeks — the opportunities begin to appear. Creative ideas come out of nowhere. Creative people show up with suggestions, or offer to assist in some way. Each opportunity seems obvious; it often seems odd that I didn't see it before. It makes me realize we are all surrounded by opportunities, all the time, but we usually don't see them, because in some way we haven't opened ourselves up to them, we haven't become receptive to them.

Doing this simple process makes us aware of opportunities, benefits, and gifts all over the place — so many that we can pick and choose between them, and do only those that are easy and relaxed, healthy and positive, for the highest good of all.

AN EXAMPLE OF THE PROCESS

Here's an example of how the process works. A while ago, I began to pray and affirm these words:

In an easy and relaxed manner,   KEY 160
in a healthy and positive way,
I am now taking a quantum leap —
personally, emotionally, and financially.

It is an unusually vague affirmation; it has no clearly defined goal. I had a sense of what I meant by "taking a personal, emotional, and financial quantum leap," though I couldn't express it more clearly than that. But it felt right to say those words. Something about the affirmation was exciting — it seemed to promise new possibilities.

After a few weeks of affirming this regularly, some opportunities came along, and things started to happen, in quick succession. Perhaps the most important thing that happened was that *The Power of Now* fell into my lap, the single best book I have ever read or published, and that book changed my life in such a way that it isn't an exaggeration to call it a quantum leap — personally, emotionally, and financially. Then four other great books came along that we published in rapid succession, and each of them in their own way helped me in taking that quantum leap.

Only a few months after I started saying that affirmation, several other very different and strong possibilities became obvious to me. I have no doubt each one would have helped as well to fulfill my goal. So I simply took the easiest and most enjoyable ones, and let the others go — and I took a quantum leap in my personal life, emotional experience, and financial life, in an easy and relaxed, healthy and positive way.

This is a common phenomenon, and worth repeating: We start affirming and then have to choose among all the possibilities. This is where the words *In an easy and relaxed manner* (etc.) come into play: If the option doesn't feel easy and relaxed, or healthy and positive, or for the highest good of all, we can let it go, and pick an option that is.

EXPERIENCE, TALENT, AND MONEY ARE NOT ESSENTIAL

The process works regardless of how much or little education you have had, or how much money, intelligence, experience, or talent you have. All those things don't matter. All the excuses you have for not succeeding are not valid. Many people with the same problems that you have succeeded brilliantly in doing what they love, once they understood what is important, what is truly essential to make this process work.

The one thing that matters, that makes all the difference in the world, is *the direction in which you focus your mind.* What matters is whether you choose to focus on the problems or on the solutions you can come up with, the opportunities in front of you, and the gifts you have.

When you work with this simple process, you plant seeds of thought and emotion in your powerful subconscious mind, and it says *Yes!* to your words and gets to work. It's worth repeating, until we know it on a deep level:

> *Your education, experience, talent, intelligence,*   KEY 161
> *and financial situation don't matter.*
> *The important thing is the direction in which you focus*
> *your unique, powerful, creative mind.*

All your old excuses don't matter any more. You are a creative being, capable of realizing your dreams. You simply have to focus on your dream, repeatedly, and then make a plan. Take the first few obvious steps in front of you, and keep taking the next steps as they become clear to you.

By doing this simple process, we align ourselves in some way with the creative forces of the universe, regardless of how well we understand those forces and regardless of the words we use to describe them.

ENVISION YOUR DEEPEST WISHES

It sounds odd and simplistic when it is put into words. I am trying to describe something I have seen and felt in my life, and it proves elusive. Maybe that's because, at its core, the process is eternally mysterious: It is the mystery of creation itself.

Whatever it is, we're an integral part of it, and can affect it and use it to fulfill our dreams. I wrote these words years ago for the beginning of a "new age symphonic rock" piece called "Overture"; the music was written by my gifted friend Sky Canyon:

KEY 162

Envision your deepest wishes
Within us are shimmering forces of creation!
Just clearly imagine whatever you wish
Within the depths of our being
is the power of realization.

A SPIRITUAL EXPLANATION

There is a force that is present everywhere, the powerful force of creation. Some call it the Creator. Some call it God. Some call it the Tao. Some call it the quantum field. Some call it chemistry, or physics.

Whatever we call it, it is present everywhere and all powerful. That means it is part of us and we are part of it. It means we wield within us great forces of creation.

KEY 163

God is omnipresent and omnipotent —
present everywhere and all powerful.
We wield tremendous forces of creation
within us.

Neither a great intelligence

nor imagination nor both together

go to the making of a genius.

Love, love, love —

that is the soul of genius.

— Wolfgang Amadeus Mozart

. . . .

THE SHORT COURSE

THE SHORT COURSE FOR ARTISTS, AND THE YOUNG, OVERWHELMED, OVERWORKED, OR HOPELESSLY LAZY

If you are an artist, or if you're young, lazy (I'm hopelessly lazy), overwhelmed, or overworked, have no fear: There's hope for you too!

If, for any reason, you can't or don't want to plow through this entire Course, here's a short version — and it may very well be all you need to dramatically improve your life.

This first section about the origin of *The Short Course* is entirely optional — feel free to skip it if you want to.

ORIGIN OF THE SHORT COURSE

After *Visionary Business* was published, a young friend of mine said, "It looks interesting — but it's, well, a book, and...." He didn't complete the sentence, just shrugged his shoulders, and it was obvious he meant he would never read something that long and involved. He asked me to summarize the book — to tell him in as few words as possible what it was about.

I ended up giving him this short Course.

He is an artist, and also completely ignorant of the business

273

. . .

world. As a result, he's a poverty case. When I think about it, he is a lot like I was when I was his age, in my twenties. I had ideas for books and I was playing music, but I had no clue how to make those things support me financially.

In many ways, I'm still a complete idiot. I meet many people who are far more intelligent than I am, far more capable, educated, sensible, and organized. Computers and machines are total mysteries to me. So is a toilet, for that matter. Once or twice I made the mistake of trying to fix a toilet — to just seat the little thingy inside so it would plug the hole in the bottom and quit running all the time — and I invariably made it far worse and had to call in someone who understood its complex mechanical mysteries.

Yet I've been able to envision (out of "thin air") the business of my dreams, and manifest it in reality — a business that supports me and many others abundantly, in a highly satisfying way.

How did I do that?

First of all, I realized that I am basically a simple person, and I need to understand things in simple language — language a five-year-old can grasp. Then I realized the process itself is simple and can be expressed in very few words. And so, for my artist friends, for myself, and for all others who could use it, here's the short version of the Course.

THE SHORT COURSE

There are four simple steps to follow that are keys to success. They are simple to explain, but can be challenging at times to put into practice. That's a good thing, though: Within the challenges and problems that arise are endless opportunities, benefits, and gifts.

1

DECIDE WHAT YOU WANT
TO DO WITH YOUR LIFE.
DECIDE TO DO WHAT YOU LOVE.

Most artists know what they want to do with their lives, but a lot of people don't. So of course it is important for us to discover what we really want to do. It is always the thing we love the most.

If money were no object, what would you do with your life?

2

DO IT, IN WHATEVER WAY YOU CAN,
AND KEEP DOING IT.
SOONER OR LATER, YOU'LL GET GOOD AT IT.

Do the thing you love to do in whatever way you can. Do it evenings, weekends, whenever you can. Watch a little less TV and do your thing instead.

Keep doing it. Do it long enough, and you'll get good at it. Every form of art and every kind of business has a craft to master. If you stick with it long enough, you'll master the craft of your art or business. Then all you need are the next two steps.

3

IMAGINE YOURSELF BEING SUCCESSFUL
DOING WHAT YOU LOVE TO DO.

Visualize your success in any way you can, as clearly as you can. This is the visionary part of this Course. Take at least a few minutes a day to imagine in whatever ways you can that you become successful doing what you love to do. Just let yourself dream; let your imagination go.

If you have trouble visualizing, take five minutes a day and brainstorm with yourself. Ask yourself how you could be successful in your art or business, and play with different possibilities that come to mind. One very effective thing to do is to make a list of several *What Ifs,* and write out different possibilities.

Keep playing with different possible scenarios, and have fun with the process. This is the stage where you're building your castle in the air — which is where it has to be at first. Feel free to let your imagination get as carried away as possible.

Let your spirit be free to dream. It all starts with a dream; then you start to imagine how that dream could possibly become a reality.

Then you find all kinds of creative ways to move — gradually and inevitably — toward your success.

4
MAKE A PLAN, AND TAKE THE FIRST OBVIOUS STEPS.

Once you've built your castle in the air, start putting a solid foundation under it. Take the first obvious steps that come along.

Eventually, make a plan: a simple, doable plan you can summarize on one or two sheets of paper. Take the next obvious steps to implement your plan.

If you continue with this, your success is inevitable. Over time, you'll create plans that will become the blueprints of your success, the architecture of your abundance.

Don't forget, in the words of James Allen in his classic book, *As You Think:*

· ·

Be not impatient in delay,   KEY 12
But wait as one who understands:
When spirit rises and commands
The gods are ready to obey.

We all have a creative spirit within us — regardless of the words we choose to describe it — and when with our will and our spirit we dream and affirm, the creative forces of the universe rush in to support us.

IT STARTS AND ENDS WITH LOVE

Do what you love to do — not only will money follow, but you'll find far greater rewards as well: satisfaction, fulfillment, even self-actualization.

Do what you love, and the greatest rewards of all will follow. You'll find yourself discovering that your life has a great and glorious purpose.

The ultimate purpose is to transform your life   KEY 165
and your world
by doing what you love to do.

THE SHORT COURSE

1

Decide what you want to do with your life.

Decide to do what you love.

2

Do it, in whatever way you can, and keep doing it.

Sooner or later, you'll get good at it.

3

Imagine yourself being successful

doing what you love to do.

4

Make a plan,

and take the first obvious steps.

. . . .

THE EXPANDED COURSE

BOOKS, AUDIO, AND VIDEO
TO ENHANCE THE COURSE

Each lesson in *The Millionaire Course* has one or more books, audios, or videos recommended to accompany it. It is certainly not necessary to work through all this material, but each one is highly recommended, because it enhances the impact of the Course.

See the Recommended Resources section that follows to find how to get each one.

THE EXPANDED COURSE

LESSON 1 *Visionary Business* by Marc Allen (book or audio)
The Visionary Business Seminar Video by Marc Allen

LESSON 2 *The One Page Business Plan* by Jim Horan

LESSON 3 *As You Think* by James Allen

LESSON 4 *The Seven Spiritual Laws of Success* by Deepak Chopra (book or audio)

LESSON 5 *The Power of Partnership* by Riane Eisler

LESSON 6 *How to Think like a Millionaire* by Mark Fisher with Marc Allen

LESSON 7 *The Power of Now* by Eckhart Tolle (book or audio)

LESSON 8 *A Visionary Life* by Marc Allen

LESSON 9 *The Architecture of All Abundance* by Lenedra J. Carroll (book or audio)

LESSON 10 *The Ten Percent Solution* by Marc Allen

LESSON 11 *Creative Visualization* by Shakti Gawain (book or audio)
The Creative Visualization Workbook by Shakti Gawain
The Bhagavad Gita: A Walkthrough for Westerners by Jack Hawley
Stress Reduction and Creative Meditations Audio by Marc Allen

LESSON 12 *A Course of Love* presented by Mari Perron and Dan Odegard

Make no small plans,

they have no magic

to stir your blood.

Make big plans,

aim high in hope and in work.

— Daniel Burnham
Designer of Golden Gate Park, San Francisco

. . . .

BOOKS, AUDIO, VIDEO

The Architecture of All Abundance by Lenedra J. Carroll (New World Library, 2001). A brilliant set of tools, filled with keys to success (see the frontispiece of this Course, page xvi).

The Art of True Healing by Israel Regardie (New World Library, 1997). A meditative journey to greater physical, emotional, and mental health.

As You Think by James Allen (New World Library, 1998). A classic work on self-empowerment, written in 1904 and absolutely current today. For over fifteen years, I felt this was the single best book I ever read. It's still right up there in the top five.

The Bhagavad Gita: A Walkthrough for Westerners by Jack Hawley (New World Library, 2001). This classic sacred work has been called "India's greatest contribution to the world." This book is in my top five as well.

Calm Surrender by Kent Nerburn (New World Library, 2000). Great advice from a great soul, told in wonderfully readable stories.

The Chalice and the Blade by Riane Eisler (HarperSanFrancisco, 1988). One of the most important books of the twentieth century. There is an excellent abridgment on audiocassette, condensed and read by the author (New World Library, 1997).

Conscious Evolution by Barbara Marx Hubbard (New World Library, 1997). Neale Donald Walsch said this was one of the eight greatest books of the twentieth century.

A Course of Love presented by Mari Perron and Dan Odegard (New World Library, 2001). Gets right to the heart, right to the essence of what is important in life, what makes life worth living. A monumental work that is spawning study groups around the country.

A Course in Miracles (Foundation for Inner Peace, 1975). A now-classic work that has inspired and changed the lives of millions.

Creating Affluence by Deepak Chopra (New World Library/Amber-Allen Publishing, 1993). Simple and brilliant.

Creative Visualization by Shakti Gawain (New World Library/Nataraj Publishing, revised edition 1995). A classic that has shown millions how to improve their lives and the world. Shakti Gawain feels *The Path of Transformation* is her best book; I feel *Creative Visualization* is. There are audio and video versions as well.

The Creative Visualization Workbook (New World Library/Nataraj Publishing, 1995). Filled with powerful hands-on exercises.

The Dynamic Laws of Prosperity by Catherine Ponder (DeVorss Publications, revised edition 1988). I believe it was from this book — though it may have been another one by the prolific Catherine Ponder — where I found the great affirmative words *"In an easy and relaxed manner, in a healthy and positive way, in its own perfect time, for the highest good of all."*

Fast Food Nation by Eric Schlosser (HarperCollins, 2002). A wake-up call. When we change our diet, we're changing the world.

The Green Money Journal — A socially and environmentally responsible magazine on business, investing, and consumer resources. (PO Box 67, Santa Fe NM 87504; (505) 988-7423; web site: www.greenmoney.com).

A Guide to Zen by Katsuki Sekida, edited by Marc Allen (New World Library, 2003). A simple, clear, and profound guide to Zen meditation.

How to Think like a Millionaire by Mark Fisher with Marc Allen (New World Library, 1997). Shows simply and clearly that wealth is a state of mind — and shows how to attain that state.

Living in the Light by Shakti Gawain (New World Library/ Nataraj Publishing, revised edition 1998), also on audio. Many people feel this is the most important work of one of our leading visionary writers and speakers.

The Living in the Light Workbook by Shakti Gawain (New World Library/Nataraj Publishing, revised edition 1998).

Living the Liberated Life by Eckhart Tolle (Namaste Publishing/ Sounds True, 2000). A transcendent talk on audiocassettes and CDs by a great modern teacher.

Letters to My Son by Kent Nerburn (New World Library, revised edition 1999). Powerful, beautifully written advice for everyone — not just someone's son.

Meditations by Shakti Gawain (New World Library/Nataraj Publishing, revised edition 2002), also on audiocassette. Highly beneficial guided meditations.

Money Magic by Deborah L. Price (New World Library, 2003). Gives you the eight money types — one of which you'll definitely identify with — and shows you how to become a "money magician." If you have issues with money, this book is great therapy.

The One Page Business Plan by Jim Horan (The One Page Business Plan Co., 1998; website: www.onepagebizplan.com). A simple and clear guide for creating short, effective plans.

The Path of Transformation by Shakti Gawain (New World Library/Nataraj Publishing, revised edition 2000). Tools for transforming our lives and healing our planet.

The Power of Now by Eckhart Tolle (New World Library, 1999). A brilliantly clear book that lives up to its subtitle: *A Guide to Spiritual Enlightenment.* If enlightenment seems too remote or impossible, this book can help you dissolve a great amount of fear, anger, and anxiety of every kind. It is already becoming a word-of-mouth classic. It's the best book I've ever read. Available on audiocassettes and CDs as well.

The Power of Partnership by Riane Eisler (New World Library, 2002). One of the most important books of the new century. If you want to improve your life or your world, read and ponder this book.

Practicing the Power of Now by Eckhart Tolle (New World Library, 2001). Essential teachings, meditations, and exercises from *The Power of Now.* A powerful work.

The Realization of Being by Eckhart Tolle (Namaste Publishing/Sounds True, 2001). A transcendent talk on audiocassette and CD that takes us beyond words. As he speaks, the pauses grow longer and longer, and he slowly, gently, and humorously guides us into the actual experience of the grace, ease, and lightness we find within when we let go of our resistance to what is.

The Richest Man in Babylon by George S. Clason (NAL-Dutton, 1988). A classic with a simple message you've heard before but probably aren't doing: Save 10 percent of your income!

The Seven Habits of Highly Effective People by Stephen R. Covey (Simon & Schuster, 1990). A classic. The second habit is a great key: Begin with the end in mind.

The Seven Spiritual Laws of Success by Deepak Chopra (New World Library/Amber-Allen Publishing, 1994). Simple yet powerful principles that can easily be applied to create success in every area of your life. A brilliant work. Available on audio.

Simple Truths by Kent Nerburn (New World Library, 1996). The work of a great soul.

Simply Living: The Spirit of the Indigenous People edited by Shirley Ann Jones (New World Library, 1999). We can learn much from the wisdom of indigenous people all over the world.

Small Graces by Kent Nerburn (New World Library, 1998). Everything by Kent Nerburn is worth reading, both for content and for his level of mastery of the craft of writing.

Stress Reduction and Creative Meditations by Marc Allen (New World Library, 1995). An audiocassette with guided meditations and affirmations that can have a powerful impact on your life.

Stress Reduction and Creative Meditations for Work and Career Audio by Marc Allen (New World Library, 1999). This audiocassette can have a wonderful effect on work and career.

The Ten Percent Solution by Marc Allen (New World Library, 2002). Filled with simple solutions to so many of the seemingly complex problems we face.

Think and Grow Rich by Napoleon Hill (Fawcett Books, 1990). The classic that has inspired millions.

Two Zen Classics: Mumonkan and Hekiganroku translated and with commentaries by Katsuki Sekida (Weatherhill, 1977). This book and *Zen Training* form a deep and complete course in Zen, written by a wonderfully self-effacing and humorous master of Zen.

Visionary Business: An Entrepreneur's Guide to Success by Marc Allen (New World Library, 1996). Filled with practical, concrete principles that show how to first imagine and then create success. Also available on audio.

The Visionary Business Workshop Video (Visionary Communications, Inc., 2003). A powerful ninety-minute seminar given by Marc Allen.

A Visionary Life: Conversations on Personal and Planetary Evolution by Marc Allen (New World Library, 1998). How to first envision and then create your deepest dreams and highest aspirations.

Work with Passion by Nancy Anderson (New World Library, revised edition 1995). How to do what you love for a living. If you're having trouble finding your passion, this is the book for you.

Zen Training by Katsuki Sekida (Weatherhill Publishers, 1975). A complete course in Zen meditation by a modern master who was a great writer as well.

RECOMMENDED RESOURCES

. . . .

WEBSITES

For information about other New World Library resources and authors, go to:

WWW.NEWWORLDLIBRARY.COM

OTHER HELPFUL WEBSITES

WWW.BOBBRINKER.COM — excellent financial advice from the host of the radio program "Moneytalk."

WWW.CHOPRA.COM — features the powerful, soul-awakening work of Deepak Chopra.

WWW.CONSCIOUSEVOLUTION.NET — gives us the wonderful work and global vision of Barbara Marx Hubbard, author of *Conscious Evolution.*

WWW.ECKHARTTOLLE.COM — more information about one of the greatest writers and speakers of our time.

WWW.GREENMONEY.COM — a guide to socially and environmentally responsible investing and business.

WWW.IDEALIST.ORG — a global coalition of individuals and organizations working to build a world where all people can live free and dignified lives in a healthy environment. Their website lists, with descriptions, over 24,000 active nonprofit groups in 153 countries.

WWW.KENTNERBURN.COM — more in-depth material about a great author.

WWW.MARCALLEN.COM — more in-depth material about the author of this book.

WWW.MONEY-THERAPY.COM — a very useful website for those who still have not mastered money featuring the work of Deborah L. Price, author of *Money Magic*.

WWW.NAMASTEPUBLISHING.COM — features the powerful, life-changing work of Eckhart Tolle, author of *The Power of Now*.

WWW.PARTNERSHIPWAY.ORG — learn how to bring partnership into every area of your life. Features the work of Riane Eisler and The Center for Partnership Studies.

WWW.SHAKTIGAWAIN.COM — more in-depth material about a writer and speaker who has had a great positive impact on the world.

SEMINARS

For information on seminars and speaking engagements of Marc Allen, go to:

WWW.MARCALLEN.COM
WWW.MILLIONAIRECOURSE.COM

ACKNOWLEDGMENTS

. . . .

To acknowledge everyone who has influenced this Course is impossible, for it includes in some meaningful way everyone I have encountered throughout the entire course of my life. We all have an impact on each other, whether we know it or not.

I have tried within the Course itself to acknowledge everyone who has had a specific, major impact on my life, and I've attempted to the best of my ability to describe what that impact has been.

But to fully acknowledge everyone who has influenced this work, I have to acknowledge everyone I've met and even all those I've never met — for we are all connected in mind and spirit, and we all influence and affect each other in countless ways we will never fully understand.

Most of all, I want to acknowledge you for reading these words at this moment. You are contributing in your own way to the evolution of humanity, and to a better world for all.

Be in peace.

. . .

INDEX

. . . .

ABOUT THE AUTHOR

. . . .

Marc Allen is co-founder (with Shakti Gawain) and president of New World Library. He has written several books, including *Visionary Business, The Ten Percent Solution,* and *A Visionary Life*. He is a popular speaker and seminar leader, and is also well known for his music. He has produced several albums, including *Solo Flight, Breathe,* and *Petals*. He lives with his family in the San Francisco Bay Area.

For more information, see these websites:

WWW.MARCALLEN.COM

WWW.NEWWORLDLIBRARY.COM

WWW.MILLIONAIRECOURSE.COM

. . .

To laugh often and love much;

To earn the respect of intelligent people

and the affection of children;

To find the best in others;

To give of oneself;

To leave the world a bit better,

whether by a healthy child,

a garden patch,

or a redeemed social condition;

To have played and laughed

with enthusiasm

and sung with exultation;

To know even one life has breathed easier

because you have lived —

this is to have succeeded.

— Ralph Waldo Emerson

New World Library
publishes books and other forms of communication
that inspire and challenge us to improve the quality
of our lives and our world.

For a catalog of our books, audios, and videos contact:

New World Library
14 Pamaron Way
Novato, CA 94949

Telephone: (415) 884-2100
Toll free: (800) 972-6657
Catalog requests: ext. 50
Ordering: ext. 52
Fax: (415) 884-2199

Email: ESCORT@NEWWORLDLIBRARY.COM
Website: WWW.NEWWORLDLIBRARY.COM

The end of all wisdom

is love,

love, love.

— Ramana Maharshi